BLACK
&
IRISH

LEON DIOP &
BRIANA FITZSIMONS

BLACK & IRISH

LEGENDS, TRAILBLAZERS & EVERYDAY HEROES

Illustrated by
JESSICA LOUIS

Little
Island

black
& irish

BLACK AND IRISH:

LEGENDS, TRAILBLAZERS AND EVERYDAY HEROES

First published in 2023 by Little Island Books, 7 Kenilworth Park, Dublin 6w, Ireland, in association with Black & Irish

First published in the USA by Little Island Books in 2024

A British Library Cataloguing in Publication record for this book is available from the British Library.

Designed and typeset by Niall McCormack

Proofread by Emma Dunne

Printed in Poland by L&C

Print ISBN: 978-1-915071-23-1

Ebook ISBN: 978-1-915071-27-9

Little Island has received funding to support this book from the Arts Council of Ireland / An Chomhairle Ealaíon

10 9 8 7 6 5 4 3 2

This book is dedicated to the Black and Mixed-Race community in Ireland. No matter how it is that you are Black and Irish, no matter where you come from, who you are, what you look like, who you love or what religion you follow, you belong here.

Contents

Introduction   page 8

Fig O'Reilly   page 13

Elliot Kwelele   page 21

Ruth Negga   page 27

Paul McGrath   page 33

Christine Buckley   page 39

Dr Monica Peres Oikeh   page 45

Boidu Sayeh   page 51

Beryl Ohas   page 57

Gavin Bazunu   page 63

Emma Dabiri   page 69

Dr Phil Mullen   page 77

Monjola   page 83

Ola Majekodunmi   page 91

Manni the Barber   page 97

Mamobo Ogoro   page 103

Phil Lynott   page 111

Blessing Dada   page 117

Lawson Mpame   page 123

Yemi Adenuga   page 129

Patrick Martins   page 137

Rhasidat Adeleke   page 143

Jude Hughes   page 149

Emer O'Neill   page 155

Dr Ebun Joseph   page 163

Dami Hope   page 167

Acknowledgements   page 172

Introduction

YOU MIGHT THINK that the idea of being Black and Irish is a relatively new thing. However, Black and Mixed-Race people have been present in Ireland for centuries, some dating as far back as the 1700s. Have you ever heard of Rachael Baptist, for example? Rachael was a Black woman from Ireland who was famous for her singing voice. She performed in concerts across Ireland and Britain, wowing crowds with her songs. She must have had some set of lungs on her!

Or how about Tom Molyneaux? He was a former slave from America who travelled to Europe to start a boxing career. He fought all over England, Scotland and Ireland in the early 1800s. He died in Galway after spending much of his life there.

And we can't talk about historic Black people in Ireland without mentioning the legendary Frederick Douglass. Frederick, an escaped slave, travelled to Ireland and recounted the horrors he faced under slavery. He became a close friend of the great Irish anti-slavery politician Daniel O'Connell, "The Liberator". Douglass recalled fondly how he was welcomed to Ireland and how the Irish treated him well.

And yet, almost 300 years later, the concept of being Black and Irish is still being discovered, discussed and even debated. It was only in the late 1990s that we saw a large influx of Black people migrating to Ireland, to work, to seek a new life and opportunities, or as asylum seekers who have had to flee their own countries. These people came to Ireland hoping for the same reception that we gave to Frederick Douglass. They brought with them new cultures, new perspectives and ultimately a new identity: the Black and Irish identity.

That is what we are here for! Black and Irish is an organisation set up to improve the quality of life for Black and Mixed-Race people in Ireland. We started in June 2020, after the murder of George Floyd in the US and the global Black Lives Matter movement that followed. We saw a massive movement kicking off around the world that shone a light on anti-Black racism. We wanted to put an Irish focus on that lens and ensure that the challenges that Black and Mixed-Race people face here were being recognised. We began as an Instagram account sharing the experience of the Black and Mixed-Race community in Ireland. And we have been working to explore Black Irish identity ever since.

We're writing this book for a few reasons. Mainly to share amazing stories, memories and experiences of some legends from the Black Irish community. There are other reasons, though. The Black Irish identity is still being formed and moulded. We believe that if you don't write your own story, then someone else will write it for you. We want to own the narrative around the formation of the Black Irish identity. So what better way to create understanding around this new identity than to share these stories with you.

We hope these stories will inspire and encourage young Black Irish people. Inspire them to follow their passions and become trailblazers; encourage them to take pride in and ownership of their identity. We also hope this book will be picked up by people from all races, creeds, ethnicities and walks of life to gain a better understanding of the Black and Irish experience.

By being Black and Irish, you are resilient. It is unfair when Black people need to work harder to get to the same level as others, but there is a certain satisfaction when you reach your goals despite having an extra mountain to climb. All of the people in this book are inspirational examples of what you can achieve when you put your mind to it. They believed in themselves. They were always open to learning. Some of them turned what other people tried to use against them into their own biggest strengths. By leaning into their Blackness and their Irishness, they empowered themselves to achieve great things.

We hope their stories will inspire you.

LEON DIOP and **BRIANA FITZSIMONS**

July 2023

Fionnghuala (Fig) O'Reilly

Miss Universe Ireland and NASA Datanaut

"Do something amazing"

WHEN FIONNGHUALA O'Reilly, better known as Fig, became the first woman of colour to win Miss Universe Ireland, with confetti flying around her as the crown was placed on her head, it was like "being awake in a dream". She remembers it as the best night of her life. But it wasn't the first time Fig experienced the joy of hard work paying off. Fig gets a lot done. She worked with NASA as a Datanaut. She's a TV correspondent. She's a model. And she's a tech startup founder.

A "Datanaut" is NASA's term for a data scientist working in the space industry.

Fig's life has always been full of variety. The daughter of a White Irish father and Black American mother who met in California, she was born on a military base in Kentucky, USA, and travelled the world as a child, never spending more than three years in any one place. This means Fig's relationship with her own identity and sense of home has always been complex.

Growing up, Fig was closely connected to her Irish extended family, which was also multi-ethnic and diverse. Having other cousins who were Mixed-Race in Ireland meant that there was always inclusivity in her family. Despite being close to her Irish relatives, Fig feels that she didn't grow up with roots anywhere.

Fig's grandfathers on both sides worked in the military and law enforcement. Her dad's dad was Deputy Garda Commissioner while her grandfather on her mother's side served in the US army. When it came time to find a career to support his growing family, Fig's father thought a structured life in the military would do the trick. Fort Knox, Kentucky was the first military base the O'Reillys found themselves living on, but this was just the start of their nomadic life.

Fig's Mixed-Race family's identity was shaped not just by their perception of themselves, but also how the world saw them. Fig can remember family meetings about which boxes to tick on forms asking about racial identity – whether it was best to tick the box for Black or White, since they weren't given the option to tick both. She also recalls many conversations with her mother and 5 sisters about how to wear their hair.

The conversation about Fig's identity has never ended. When she won Miss Universe Ireland, she was the first woman of colour to do so. Despite this amazing achievement, Fig felt

Abeeb Yusuf

Abeeb Yusuf is a social media star, model, content creator and tech professional based in Dublin. Most famous for his styling videos, Abeeb is known for his ability to make high-street, everyday fashion look like luxury.

Between his Instagram and TikTok accounts, Abeeb's videos are informative, giving followers valuable tips about where to buy the latest styles, as well as how much they cost. He mixes music, fashion and humour, all while playfully showing his followers how easy it is to use everyday fashions to dress to impress. Whether you're looking for inspiration on outfits for dates, shopping or job interviews, Abeeb's advice can help get you looking your best.

Abeeb also works in the technology industry as a development coordinator, proving that he is a man of many talents.

like she had to defend her identity yet again. At the age of 25, she was confident in both her Black and Irish identities, but now that the spotlight was on her, people started questioning them. There were many who accepted her understanding of her identity, but others didn't. Despite having done so much work to understand her own identity, when such a personal thing as her race was questioned, it was incredibly difficult for Fig.

Since she moved around so much growing up, there were only two really consistent things in Fig's life: sports and school. Sports were fun and a way to meet people her own age, but they also taught her dedication and the importance of hard work. Fig viewed school as the key to success and a way out of the food-insecure household of her teen years. After her parents had split up, her mother worked hard to provide her daughters with everything they needed, but as a single parent, it wasn't always easy.

Traditionally **STEM** (Science, Technology, Engineering, and Maths) subjects have been more commonly studied by male students. Today many women in STEM, like Fig, are working to break down this stereotype and encourage more girls to consider taking STEM subjects in school and university.

When Fig was 14 her maths teacher realised that Fig had the potential to do something great with her maths ability. He recommended Fig for a three-year summer programme in STEM for low-income students of colour at University of California, Berkeley. This opportunity brought her life down a completely new path. It was in this programme that she learned about engineering, learned productivity and time management skills, and learned about the path of academic achievement.

Fig went to college on a Navy scholarship with the goal of becoming a pilot in the US Navy and ultimately an astronaut. She went to George Washington University in Washington DC and studied systems engineering, despite never having visited the school or the city before. At college Fig decided to join every club and student society that she could. One of these was the Miss Freshmen Pageant, which was her first experience of pageantry. At the same time, she also found a supportive community by becoming a member of a historically Black sorority, Alpha Kappa Alpha Sorority, Inc. As a member of Alpha Kappa Alpha, Fig began her journey in community and volunteering work, and has never stopped working to uplift and advance the Black community.

Sororities are all-female societies at American universities. They can offer students scholarships, housing and connections for life. The male equivalents are fraternities. **ALPHA KAPPA ALPHA SORORITY, INC.**, was the first all-Black sorority. It has a history of over 100 years of commitment to service, sisterhood and scholarship.

Her experience with pageants ultimately led Fig to enter Miss Universe Ireland, which she describes as a rollercoaster. Pageants are all about the beauty and the show that everyone gets to see, but a lot of effort goes on behind the scenes. When all of her hard work culminated in the beautiful experience of being crowned Miss Universe Ireland, it was the best night of Fig's life. She will never forget her name being called as winner while 17 members of her family watched from the audience. They held up light-up letters spelling her full name, F-I-O-N-N-G-H-U-A-L-A, so that she could see them among the crowd.

Fig loved her time as Miss Universe Ireland. While she loved the photoshoots and glamour that came with the title, she equally enjoyed having the opportunity to speak at events about issues that mattered to her, like advocating for women in STEM. She felt the responsibility to do her best to hold the door open for other girls and women of colour to come in behind her. Fig was well aware of the weight of her win, being the first person of colour to win a pageant after 60 years of pageantry in Ireland. She wanted to do her best to represent Ireland, but she also wanted to uplift and hold space for other women.

The **BLACK LIVES MATTER** movement kicked off in response to the terrible killing of a Black man named George Floyd by a policeman in the USA in 2020. The movement spread around the world and in Ireland protestors took to the streets in solidarity and to raise awareness of anti-Black racism in Ireland and around the world.

In the wake of the murder of George Floyd in 2020, Fig joined Black Lives Matter protests in Dublin and used her platform to bring awareness to the Black experience in Ireland. Even then, she found her identity was questioned by others. She was unprepared for some hurtful things that were said about her by members of the Black Irish community because she is a light-skinned Black woman.

SPACE TO REACH, Fig's tech startup, was founded in 2022. Their mission is to "build a pathway for more women of colour to excel in innovation-driven industries". You can learn more about the company at spacetoreach.com.

While she was surprised by the backlash that she experienced from within her own community, she never stopped advocating for Black women everywhere. For Fig, Blackness is not a "monolith" – there are many different experiences and different identities within Blackness, and Fig knows that she could not take on or represent all of the difficulties and experiences of the wider Black diaspora.

Today Fig is a systems engineer and works in the field of data science. She spent two years working with NASA as a "Datanaut", and was the Director of NASA's Space Apps Challenge, which is an international hack-a-thon. She has also founded a tech startup called Space to Reach which works to close the opportunity gap for Black and Brown women in STEM. Fig's travel hasn't stopped in her adult years and she only recently moved back to the US to work on a television show called *Mission Unstoppable* – but she can't wait to return to Ireland soon.

Young people in Ireland today are the most diverse generation ever seen in the country. Fig says she loves to see "the beauty in their colourful rainbow" and believes today's young Irish people will do some amazing things for this country in the very near future. One of Fig's biggest hopes for Ireland is that systems will be put in place that demand equality for everyone. She believes that Ireland is in a unique position to build-in representation and equality right now and make sure to include and respect everyone in our society.

Elliot Kwelele

Irish dancing champion

"Immerse yourself in life"

ELLIOT KWELELE is the top-ranked Irish dancer in the world in his age category. At just 17 years old, he has won the World Irish Dancing Championships twice. You might be asking yourself, how did a Nigerian-Irish lad from Dundalk end up at the top of the world in a traditional ultra-competitive sport like Irish dancing?

IRISH DANCING is a traditional form of dancing in Ireland and is usually accompanied by traditional music. It is practised socially at *céilí* dances and competitively in Ireland and internationally.

Elliot was born in Dundalk after his parents emigrated to Ireland from Nigeria. He is a middle child in an all-boy household. When he was growing up, his dad stayed at home to look after his youngest brother, who is disabled. Elliot sees that as an amazing example of how sacrifices are sometimes necessary to take care of the ones we love. He takes inspiration from his brother's story of survival. Elliot's mother, a community healthcare worker, also gave him an example of what it means to look after others.

It's safe to say Elliot has a lot of role models to look up to. He isn't the only athlete in the family: one of his older brothers plays professional soccer while also attending university.

Elliot says that his parents brought him and his brothers up with love and care and that they showed them the "essence of life": not to take things for granted and to always try their best. They taught him to "immerse himself in life" and follow his passions to the fullest. He believes in God and says that it's important to be thankful for each day and see everything you have as a blessing.

Elliot was one of very few Black students in primary school but his secondary school was a bit more diverse. He always felt that he had to work twice as hard as other students, both in school and in dancing, because of his Blackness. He feels that if he makes any mistakes they are more likely to be noticed because he stands out. His Blackness makes him unique in the world of Irish dancing, and while that can be a positive, it also makes him a target. Elliot is proud to represent not only Irish culture with his dancing, but also the Black Irish community, which means that he feels the pressure to do well.

It was during a recital in primary school on St Patrick's Day that Elliot first encountered Irish dancing. He fell in love with the music and was entranced by the way the performers moved on stage. Afterwards he asked his school friends to show him some steps out on the yard. He was so fascinated by it that he went home and, at age 9, told his parents that he wanted to start Irish dancing classes.

Elliot's parents knew he would be the only Black person in the classes and were concerned he might get some negative criticism which could affect young Elliot's mental health. They also noticed that there weren't many boys enrolled in classes, although they knew of the icon Michael Flatley from *Riverdance*. Reassured by Elliot's conviction and drive to try something new that he was passionate about, his parents agreed. Elliot knew right away that he wanted to be the best at competitive and professional Irish dancing, so he decided to quit playing football and put all of his effort into dancing.

RIVERDANCE is an Irish dancing troupe and show which originally starred probably the most famous Irish dancer ever, the Irish-American Michael Flatley. It was first performed as part of the Eurovision Song Contest when it was held in Ireland, and has since became a worldwide phenomenon.

Elliot has gone on to win the World Championships twice, in back-to-back competitions, along with winning the All-Ireland Championships twice, three Irish National Championships, and five Ulster Regional Oireachtas titles. He is incredibly proud of his accomplishments to date, and the fact that he did it all without having a role model who looked like him to look up to. Elliot is motivated by the public reaction and support that he's got from his success. He knows that he can continue to be successful and achieve even more.

There are three levels of Irish dancing: beginners, preliminary and championship level. Once you've moved through the levels, you can take it on as a career or become a dance instructor. There are also opportunities for judging *feiseanna*, or competitions.

In addition to his achievements at competition level, Elliot has also danced on *The Late Late Toy Show*. In 2017, he was honoured in his home town when he received a Civic Award in Dundalk for his achievements in dance. He was the youngest dancer to ever perform with the *Riverdance* dancers, as well as being the first person of colour to do so. Last year he was accepted into the *Riverdance* troupe as a professional dancer.

Elliot firmly puts Irish dancing in the "sport" category based on the effort, time and sacrifice that is required to compete. Personally, he has dedicated a lot of time and energy to the sport, often missing out on events and opportunities that other young people take part in, all in the pursuit of his dream of being the best. There have been many highs and lows, but Elliot lives by the saying "hard work beats talent when talent doesn't work hard".

Elliot recently graduated from secondary school as the top

student in his class. He won Student of the Year and multiple science, French and other academic awards. He is incredibly proud of these achievements. He feels that he represents not only himself with those successes, but also the Black Irish community.

Elliot hopes to go on to study medicine and become a doctor. He would like to have an enjoyable lifestyle and a professional career he enjoys, but he also wants to be known for his contribution to Irish dancing. He wants to inspire others to see how discipline and determination can help them achieve their goals. He believes that he will be successful at anything he puts his mind to, and he's definitely shown that to be true!

Ruth Charles

Ruth Charles is a Mixed-Race woman from Dublin. She is a professional Irish dancer currently touring with *Riverdance*, which has been her dream since she was a young girl.

Ruth began dancing at the age of 4. Growing up, she danced competitively and was crowned Leinster champion three times and placed 12th in the World Championships. She became a professional dancer at the age of 22. She was the lead dancer in shows called *Celtic Legends* and *Celtic Gold*, performing in countries around the world, before joining the legendary Michael Flatley's *Feet of Flames* show for a tour of Taiwan in 2020.

Ruth's motto is "aspire to inspire". Her advice for young Black Irish dancers is: "Your skin tone doesn't mean that there's a limit to the successes you can achieve. Work hard, dream big and let your dancing do the talking."

Elliot believes that Ireland is changing and progressively getting better. As a young person, he would like to see Ireland become more inclusive. He'd like to see both education and healthcare become more accessible for those who are disadvantaged. While he doesn't see himself pursuing a career in politics, Elliot wants to be an advocate for change. He hopes to use his platform to advocate for inclusivity in Irish dance, especially for young Black people.

If you have any hopes or aspirations in dance, Elliot says, "Go and do it! You are not alone. If I can do it, you can do it too!" Setbacks and low points will happen, but it's how you respond to those negative moments that makes you great. Elliot wants young people to know themselves and mind themselves throughout life's highs and lows, and to remember where they come from and know their roots. His work now is all about striving for the best for the generation that will come next. If he can be an example for the next generation of dancers, he says, "that's more than enough for me".

Ruth Negga

A Black Irish actress in Hollywood

"Allow your courage to be bigger than your fear"

WHEN RUTH NEGGA was a young girl in Limerick in the west of Ireland, she and her cousin made a pact: if either of them were ever nominated for an Oscar, they would bring the other to the ceremony as their date. Decades later Ruth brought her cousin to the Academy Awards in Hollywood when she was nominated for the Best Actress Oscar for her role in the movie *Loving*.

Ruth always wanted to act. Today she lives in Los Angeles and is one of Ireland's most successful actors. In addition to the Oscar nomination, she has been nominated for a Golden Globe, starred on Irish screens in the hit gangland drama *Love/Hate* and appeared in the Marvel TV series *Agents of S.H.I.E.L.D.* In 2022 she made her Broadway debut in a production of Shakespeare's *Macbeth* as Lady Macbeth, opposite James Bond actor Daniel Craig.

Ruth was born in Ethiopia to an Irish mother and Ethiopian father and spent the first couple of years of her life there. Her mother was a nurse and her father was a doctor. They met in a hospital in Ethiopia when Ruth's mother was working as a nurse for the Irish charity Concern.

Civil war raged in Ethiopia from 1974 to 1991, fought between supporters and opponents of a Communist regime that had seized power from the Emperor Haile Selassie. During this time a terrible famine broke out, which may have killed as many as 1.2 million people and caused 400,000 to flee as refugees.

Ruth's mother took her back to Ireland when serious civil unrest broke out in Ethiopia. Her father was not permitted to leave the country as the Communist regime was trying to stop a "brain drain" – the emigration of highly educated and skilled workers. Her father planned to find a way to follow them to Ireland, but he died in an accident before he had the chance to be reunited with his family. This loss has led to Ruth feeling disconnected from her African heritage. This is something she has had to work on herself and learn about in her own time.

Ruth had a positive experience growing up in Limerick. She lived on the same road as many of her family members, so there were always cousins around to hang out with. The people around her accepted her and didn't make her feel different because of the colour of her skin. To her, Limerick was home and she didn't feel different to anyone else. Her family raised her to believe that she could be or do anything.

When Ruth grew up there weren't many Black or Mixed-Race people around, and she believes that White Irish people

Jade Jordan

Jade Jordan is a Mixed-Race actor from North Dublin. Jade's notable achievements include appearing in several movies and on the stage of the Abbey Theatre, Ireland's national theatre.

Jade is also an author. Her book *Nanny, Ma and Me* tells the story of her grandmother Kathleen, her mother Dominique and her own experiences growing up as a Black woman in Ireland. Her grandmother moved from Ireland to Britain in the 1950s, where she met and married a Jamaican man. She then returned to Ireland with three Mixed-Race children, one of whom is Jade's mother. Jade's mother came to Ireland in her teens and had to navigate a difficult time on account of being Mixed-Race.

Jade continues to make strides. In 2021 she wrote, produced and starred in her own short film, *The Colour Between*.

may have been more accepting of Black people when she was young. When there is only a small number of people from a different background, then they are not seen as a threat. Today in Ireland we are seeing increasing protests against immigrants. Ruth believes this is because the number of immigrants has increased to the point that some people feel threatened.

Ruth had her first serious encounters with racism when she moved to London to attend secondary school. It was there that she had what she calls a "lifting of the veil moment". This was when she realised she wasn't the same as other people: that she was Black and most people around her were White. During Ruth's time in London, the murder of a Black teenager named Steven Lawrence was in the news. This incident had a profound effect on her. It showed her how strong racism was in the UK at the time. To this day she gets emotional while thinking or talking about it.

Steven Lawrence was a Black British teenager who was killed in a racially motivated attack while he was standing at a bus stop in 1993 in London. Despite a number of eyewitnesses and suspects, no one was convicted of the murder for many years. This led to an inquiry which concluded that London's Metropolitan Police Service was institutionally racist. The incident led to significant changes in the way the police handle race-related crimes in the UK.

Fortunately Ruth never had any violent encounters but she did experience racism based on both her Blackness *and* her Irishness. It was thanks to the strong sense of self that her family instilled in her that she was able to believe in herself and not allow the prejudice to stop her from doing what she had always dreamed of: acting.

After appearing in some plays in London, Ruth decided to come home to Ireland and study acting at Trinity College Dublin. Trinity's illustrious campus and history attracted her. She loves history and would have studied it if she hadn't gone into acting. She reckons she was lucky to have come home to study. In the UK she would have been put in a box and only given certain narrow acting roles, such as the "Black best friend". But in Ireland her talent was recognised and she was given great opportunities. Straight out of college, she landed the role of Lolita in a hugely successful stage production based on the classic novel *Lolita*.

Later Ruth moved to America. She never had a strict plan in her mind, which allowed her to pivot when she needed to. As she was building her career, she felt like she had a constant dynamo inside her, driving her on from one project to the next. Despite this, she always allows herself time to celebrate her wins, which she thinks is important.

One of the best things Ruth has done for herself was letting go of the fear of failure. Becoming friends with failure helped her to push herself out of her comfort zone. Things happen in the world of acting that you won't be prepared for. Ruth was cast by director Steve McQueen in his film *12 Years a Slave*, which went on to win the Best Picture Oscar. After filming her part, she received a call from McQueen letting her know that she wasn't included in the final cut of the movie. While this was devastating at the time, Ruth

Ruth's advice to young actors is to be true to yourself and trust yourself. Find an internal security within yourself and don't allow anyone to steal that from you. If you have a bad feeling about something, trust your gut and don't do it. Allow your courage to be bigger than your fear. And don't be in a rush. Ruth believes in longevity and says that to avoid being a flash in the pan, you need work with your own internal rhythm.

knew that it was just part of the game and she would have to get over it. She is resilient and knows that, while these things hurt at the time, they don't last.

Today Ruth is a world-renowned actor and she gives back to her community in many ways. She is a patron of A Partnership with Africa, an Irish charity which supports a partnership-based approach to development in countries in Africa. She is also an ambassador for the Catalyst International Film Festival, a Limerick-based festival committed to addressing the underrepresentation of minorities in the film industry.

Paul McGrath

Professional footballer

"The Black Pearl of Inchicore"

"OOH AHH, Paul McGrath, I said ooh ahh Paul McGrath!" This song has been sung around the world to celebrate the talent of a special Irish person. Paul McGrath is a former professional footballer who played for Ireland during its golden era. He was a star player in the only Ireland team to reach a World Cup quarter-final, and played for major English clubs including Manchester United. At a time when there weren't many Irish people of colour in the limelight, Paul was an iconic figure.

Paul's mother was Irish and his father was Nigerian. They met when his father was a medical student in Dublin. His father left his mother to have the baby alone, in 1959, a time when an unmarried woman having a baby was considered deeply scandalous. She travelled to London to have her baby in secret. Paul ended up in an orphanage in Ireland. Fortunately he and his mother later had a close relationship. Living in the orphanage was tough. There were often fights between the kids. However, it was there that Paul fell in love with football.

> "Paul had this really nonchalant way of defending. [...] A ball would come into the box and he'd just back-heel it to safety." — Paul's Manchester United manager, Sir Alex Ferguson

Paul began his career playing for local football clubs. He was discovered by a man named Tommy Heffernan who brought him to Pearse Rovers. He scored 4 goals in his first match! He later joined Dalkey United at the age of 17, where he became a defender. He went on to play for Dublin's St Patrick's Athletic before joining Manchester United in 1982. At United he established himself as a top-class central defender. He played for the club for 7 years, winning the FA Cup in 1985. That same year Paul made his debut for Ireland. He went on to earn 83 caps, scoring 8 goals. He was a crucial part of Jack Charlton's Irish team, which was successful beyond the wildest dreams of Ireland fans at the time.

In 1990 Ireland qualified for the World Cup in Italy, Ireland's first ever World Cup, with Paul McGrath at the heart of the defence. They reached the quarter-final, where they lost to Italy. Four years later Ireland had the chance for revenge. They again qualified for the World Cup, USA '94, and played Italy in their first match, at Giants Stadium in New Jersey.

At that time Italian football was regarded by many as the best in the world, and Italy went on to finish runner-up in the tournament. Their star player was the forward Roberto Baggio. Paul marked Baggio and gave the performance of his life, making a series of world-class blocks and tackles that prevented the superstar from influencing the match. Ireland shocked the world by winning 1–0. To this day Paul's performance is regarded as one of the best ever seen in an Irish shirt. He subsequently revealed that he was carrying a painful shoulder injury in the match, which had almost kept him out of the game.

"Big Paul McGrath showed all the qualities demanded of us [...] in Giants Stadium that day. [...] When the Italians did get sight of the goal, Paul presented a final, insurmountable obstacle." — Paul's Ireland teammate Roy Keane

The **ITALIA '90** World Cup was a historic moment in Irish sport. Despite never having qualified for a World Cup before, Ireland reached the quarter-finals, where they were narrowly defeated by the host nation. Four years later Ireland again qualified. Paul McGrath was a key part of both teams, which also included players such as familiar TV pundits Roy Keane, Ray Houghton and Ronnie Whelan.

At Manchester United, Paul was a key player in the team that won the FA Cup in 1985. The following season, legendary manager Alex Ferguson took over the club. Ferguson and Paul didn't get on and the manager transferred him to Aston Villa in 1989. He later revealed that Ferguson had offered him £100,000 (a huge amount of money at that time) to retire immediately! But years later, Ferguson spoke of his admiration for Paul's ability, and poetically described him as having "an athleticism that was musical". Ferguson helped Paul to find work at Manchester United after he retired from playing.

Aston Villa fans still sing Paul McGrath's name at matches and refer to him as "God"!

Chris Hughton

Chris Hughton was the first Black player to represent Ireland. His mother was White Irish and his father was from Ghana. A full-back, Hughton played most of his club career at Tottenham Hotspur. He won the FA Cup twice and the UEFA Cup (what is today called the Europa League) with Spurs.

Chris played at Ireland's first ever international tournament, Euro '88 in Germany, where Ireland beat England in their first match, and was part of the legendary Italia '90 squad along with Paul McGrath.

After he retired from playing, Chris went into coaching and was the Ireland assistant manager under Brian Kerr from 2003–05. He has managed clubs including Newcastle and Brighton. In 2023 he became the manager of the Ghana national team. His son, Cian Hughton, played for Ireland under-21s.

Paul helped Aston Villa become one of the best teams in England, twice finishing second in the Premier League and winning the League Cup in 1994. He was named the PFA (Professional Footballer's Association) Player of the Year for the 1992–93 season. Voted for by fellow footballers, and chosen from all the players in the league that year, that is one of the highest honours a Premier League footballer can earn, and it is very unusual for a defender to win it.

Paul later played for Derby County and Sheffield United. For much of his career he struggled with knee injuries, often playing through pain, and towards the end he was unable to train between matches. Nonetheless he could still put in top-level performances until his retirement aged 38.

Despite his success on the field, Paul struggled with a number of off-field issues, including a difficult battle with alcoholism. In his autobiography *Back from the Brink* he describes points in his life when his struggles brought him very low. Several football managers took responsibility for helping Paul, and the Ireland manager Jack Charlton became a sort of father figure to him.

"My all-time favourite Manchester United footballer has to be without any shadow of a doubt, Paul McGrath. [...] I loved and still cherish every minute of every game I had the honour and privilege of playing alongside Paul in the red of United and the green of Ireland." — Paul's fellow centre-back from Dublin, Kevin Moran

As a player Paul was known for his strong tackling and aerial ability, as well as his ability to read the game and anticipate the opposition's movements. He was widely considered one of the best defenders of his generation. One of the most amazing things about Paul's career is that he was able to perform at an elite level even when he was struggling with addiction.

Paul McGrath was a major figure in Irish sporting life at a time when there were not many Black or Mixed-Race public figures in the country. He had a few Black teammates for Ireland, such as Chris Hughton, Terry Phelan and Phil Babb, but none that reached his level of fame or adulation. Today there are many more Black and Mixed-Race Irish footballers, but Paul was a trailblazer. His example showed how a Black player could win the hearts of Irish fans, and he helped to convince White Irish people that Black and Irish identity was not a contradiction but something real.

Christine Buckley

Justice campaigner for survivors of state institutions

"Her legacy lives on"

CHRISTINE BUCKLEY was abandoned by her parents at three weeks old and grew up in an industrial school. Like many others, she experienced the horrors and cruelty of that system. She did not allow this trauma to stop her from becoming a qualified nurse and going on to fight for others like her. Her advocacy has changed the lives of many people who grew up in the cruel industrial school system in Ireland. She inspired many people to take up the mantle of activism, including her own family members.

INDUSTRIAL SCHOOLS were institutions that provided homes and education for "neglected, orphaned and abandoned children". The schools were notorious in Ireland for cruelty. An investigation concluded in 2009 that a lot of abuse occurred in industrial schools.

Christine was born in London in 1946 to an Irish mother and a Nigerian father. This was considered an affair because her mother was married but separated – at that time in Ireland there was no divorce – and it was deeply scandalous for people to have children outside of marriage. At 4 years of age, Christine was sent to live in St Vincent's Industrial School in Goldenbridge, Dublin. She described it as being like living in hell.

Every Saturday, Christine was visited by a White woman and a Black man. She would be dressed up and would wait for them to arrive. She wondered if they were her parents. She later learned that the man was her father, but the woman was not her mother. One Saturday, she waited and waited. They never came back.

Christine faced a lot of racial abuse at the industrial school. She was called names and slurs often. Christine and others in the school were forced to make rosary beads. If they didn't hit their daily target of beads, they weren't allowed to eat or sleep until they finished the work. It was common to get cuts, splinters and pains in their hands or eyes from making the beads.

One day, Christine decided to try to stop all of the abuses that were happening in the industrial school. She wrote a letter and

Conor Buckley

Son of Christine, Conor Buckley's childhood was deeply rooted in morality and activism as he witnessed his mother go head-to-head with the state and church regarding abuses in state-run institutions. Today Conor is an activist and campaigner and founder of Human Collective, an award-winning sustainable clothing brand that has a mission to spread a message of equality and unity. He also runs anti-discrimination workshops teaching young people about discrimination and bias and has made TV appearances to talk about discrimination.

The Human Collective believes in the principle of "universal inclusion", that there is only one race – the human race – and that we all have the responsibility to make the world and our workplace more inclusive. Its logo is an equals sign, representing equality. The Human Collective is on a quest to get people to "wear what they believe" and show allyship and support for racial equality, opportunity equality, LGBTQIA+ equality and gender equality. For every sale of its clothing the Human Collective donates money to three different charities: LGBT Ireland, SARI (Sport Against Racism Ireland) and the Irish Youth Foundation.

passed it to someone outside of the school. Unfortunately the letter was returned to the school and the school directors were furious. They rounded everyone in the school up and informed them that they would all be punished until the person who wrote the letter came forward. Not wanting anyone else to suffer, Christine confessed to writing the letter. She was badly beaten and her leg was severely injured in the process. She required more than a hundred stitches for her leg. This is one of the countless incidences of cruelty inflicted on Christine in the industrial home.

Rosary beads are used by some Christians (mostly Roman Catholics) to say prayers. Some of the industrial schools operated as rosary-bead factories, forcing the children to make beads for sale. Investigations have found that the money made from selling the beads was spent by the schools.

At the age of 18 Christine left St Vincent's. While she had been waiting over 13 years for this, she recalled that it was quite a sad day. Two years earlier the school had been taken over by a new head nun who transformed the lives of the people living there for the better. Christine would go on to qualify as a nurse which was uncommon for people in her situation. She trained as a nurse in Drogheda and while there she received her birth certificate. This was the first official paper she had confirming her identity.

Christine married Donal Buckley and had three children, Cliona, Darragh and Conor. After her third child, Christine was diagnosed with cervical cancer. She promised herself that as soon as she recovered and got her strength back, she would begin the search for her parents. It was very difficult but eventually she found them both. She told this story through the powerful documentary *Dear Daughter*. The documentary highlighted the

Conrad Bryan

Conrad Bryan was born in 1964 and grew up in Irish childcare institutions. Like many children born outside marriage he was considered "illegitimate". The stigma of this status was compounded by the fact that his father was African. Conrad was considered unsuitable for family life due to his colour and therefore he was never placed for adoption.

When he was a kid, Conrad would often wonder about his biological parents, even wondering if his father was a king. He eventually found out his father's name and learned that he was a South African doctor who had been living in England. Unfortunately, by this time his father had passed away, but the rest of Conrad's extended African family warmly welcomed him, filling a gap in his identity.

Conrad recently graduated with a master's degree in Human Rights Law. In May 2023, he spoke in the United Nations General Assembly Hall in New York, calling for justice and reparations for the racial discrimination Mixed-Race children experienced in Irish Mother-and-Baby Homes and Industrial Schools. He is a founding Director of The Association of Mixed Race Irish and continues to explore legal action at the UN.

MOTHER-AND-BABY HOMES in Ireland were institutions where unmarried pregnant women were sent to have their "illegitimate" babies. The women lived in the homes for a time afterwards and suffered a lot of cruelty, and were forced to do hard manual work. Their children were typically put up for adoption or sent to live in institutions.

abuses that Christine and others faced in the industrial schools. It also told the story of her life. It made a huge contribution to the Irish public becoming aware of what had gone on in the industrial schools.

In 1992, Christine Buckley co-founded the Aislinn Education and Support Centre in Dublin. The centre provided support and assistance to those who had experienced abuse in industrial schools and other institutions. Through her work at Aislinn, Christine became a powerful voice for survivors, advocating for their rights and working to expose the harsh realities of their experiences.

In 1999, the Taoiseach at the time, Bertie Ahern, made a public apology to the survivors of the industrial schools system. He partly credited this apology to meeting Christine and hearing her story.

Christine continued to campaign for justice for survivors of institutional abuse throughout her life. She worked closely with the Irish government's Commission to Inquire into Child Abuse. In 2009 that commission published the Ryan Report, which revealed widespread physical, emotional and sexual abuse suffered by thousands of children in Irish institutions over several decades. Christine's work helped pave the way for the Residential Institutions Redress Board, which provided compensation to survivors of abuse.

Christine passed away in 2014. Her legacy lives on through her children and colleagues and admirers who have followed in her footsteps.

Dr Monica Peres Oikeh

Doctor and social media star

"Changing the face of medicine"

DR MONICA PERES OIKEH is a full-time general practitioner (GP) doctor who has a TikTok account with over 60 thousand followers. Monica delivers information about health, especially women's health, through social media. She also describes herself as a dog-mom who has a newfound passion for animals and their health.

Monica moved to Ireland from Nigeria after her mother died when Monica was just 15 years old. She had never heard of Ireland before she came here to live with her father, stepmother and siblings. She didn't know what to expect when she arrived. One of her first memories of being in awe of Ireland was when her father took her for a drive through the Phoenix Park in Dublin. She couldn't believe the beauty of so much nature right in the middle of the city. She loved it.

Monica's posts about health are on TikTok at @dr.blondieperes and Instagram at @blondieperes

The first time Monica saw snow was during a physics class in school and she remembers wanting to go out and experience it first-hand, but feeling shy. She also recalls thinking that the houses in Ireland were much smaller than she was accustomed to. The fact that there were very few gates in front of the houses also made her feel safe because it meant there wasn't as much need for protection as there had been in Nigeria.

When she started school in Blakestown in Dublin, Monica found it difficult to understand her teachers' Irish accents. For the first three months it sounded to her like the teachers were "singing". Her first set of exam results were not stellar. But once she got the hang of things her grades went right up. Monica's teachers began to focus on her and help her to do her very best.

Monica recalls comments from classmates about her accent and was asked often, "Why do you speak like that?" She remembers explaining that she grew up speaking English in Nigeria and that there are many places around the world that, like Ireland, were colonised by the British, and so people in those places speak English with different accents.

Monica was never able to integrate herself into the Irish way of speaking and she didn't adapt her accent to sound more like Irish people. Comments about her accent happened so frequently that Monica began to feel "really small" and it affected her confidence. She was also criticised frequently about her fashion sense. That is often just part of being a teenager, but coming from another country and being so different didn't make her teenage years any easier. Monica's free time was spent mostly in the library, surrounded by books, which was easier than dealing with negative criticism from her peers.

English is the official language of Nigeria. There are over 500 other languages spoken in the country. Nigeria was a colony of Britain from the mid-19th century until 1960 when it gained its independence.

Monica was the only Black student out of 180 people in her medicine course at Trinity College, Dublin. Still affected by the criticisms from her youth, Monica struggled to speak to her classmates and get to know those around her. She had to work to support herself through college, doing two or three jobs at any given time, because she didn't qualify for the grants that other students were eligible for, since she had relatively recently arrived in the country.

At college Monica joined the Afro-Caribbean Society. She is proud of working on the launch of the first Intercultural Christmas

Party together with the other international societies on campus. She joined a mentoring society to partner with incoming first-year students and help them through the transition into college life, which she had found difficult. She also joined Solas, an organisation that supports refugees, despite often being mistaken for a refugee herself.

Monica knew that she wanted to be a GP early on in her studies because she really liked the holistic, or whole-person, approach to healthcare that the job would give her, as opposed to other types of doctoring which are more specialised.

Monica's proudest moment is her graduation from university. When she heard that she had passed her exams she was in disbelief. She had had so much self-doubt, she had convinced herself that she was not really capable of doing well. She now realises that she was suffering from "imposter syndrome".

IMPOSTER SYNDROME is a feeling that the success you have is not real, that you don't deserve it, that you are a fraud or a phony – an imposter pretending to be somebody successful. People with imposter syndrome can feel anxious that their achievements will be taken away from them and they'll be exposed as frauds. This can be experienced even by very successful people.

When Monica came to Ireland, it wasn't "cool" to be Black, and she didn't feel like she could be her true self around others. She sees things changing in Ireland and feels hopeful because being Black and Irish is being celebrated now. It gives her joy to see Black Irish kids embracing their dual identity and being involved in Irish culture through sport and music, and being celebrated for their contributions to Irish society.

For Monica, being Black and Irish is about appreciating the culture of your ancestors or where you were born, while also loving the Irish part of you by fully embracing everything that comes with being Irish. It's not about being "either this or that" but having the two parts make a whole: you can be Black *and* Irish. Monica says that there is no conflict between the two parts of her and that she enjoy both identities at the same time.

Monica didn't set out to get tons of followers when she started using social media. She was just excited to share her story. She hadn't realised how few Black Irish GPs there were until she started meeting patients who were surprised to see her in the role, and their reactions were often quite positive and even funny. She wanted to share these experiences with others as well as get the word out about practical medical advice.

Monica's mother passed away due to medical negligence. Her mother's death gave Monica the drive to study medicine. She wanted to help prevent similar deaths in the world and save other children from going through what she had.

When she started out working as a GP, Monica saw very few Black patients coming to her practice in Cork. She wondered if it was because there were so few Black doctors.

When she did encounter Black patients, she could see their joy in finding someone like themselves looking after them. Monica believes this was because Black patients felt that a Black doctor would be more inclined to listen to and understand them. This drove her to use social media to get the word out about important medical advice, especially for people in the Black Irish community.

During the COVID-19 pandemic Monica discovered TikTok. It was her young patients who inspired her to share Irish-specific advice using that platform, which was already saturated with advice from countries like the USA and the UK. From there, she started getting approached by companies that wanted to support her work while also have her advocate for their services. Monica recently participated in a TV programme called *The Clinic for Well People*, where a team of medical professionals assessed just how healthy seemingly well people actually were.

Monica hopes that her story encourages young people to pursue their passions, because at the end of the day, work's not just about the money, it's about following your heart. And you never know how lucrative your passion might be in the long run. Monica hopes that her presence in the medical field will help more people receive medical advice and assistance. She knows that it can be difficult to feel misunderstood by doctors, who may not always empathise with the situations of people who are different from them, but she hopes that she represents a change in the profession, a change for the better.

Monica's plans for the future include owning her own GP practice and continuing on her social media journey, possibly creating a podcast and writing a book. She wants to keep putting herself out there and making positive changes for the Black community in Ireland.

It's important for everyone to feel like they can go to their GP whenever they feel the need and not just wait until they are unwell. More Black doctors in GP practices around the country will help encourage Black people to go to the doctor when necessary and make medical care more accessible for the Black community. Hopefully many more young Black Irish people will enter the medical field and continue to change the face of medicine in the country.

Boidu Sayeh

Westmeath Gaelic football player

"Bringing diversity, love and kindness into the GAA"

BOIDU SAYEH, star corner-back for the Westmeath Gaelic football team, says that growing up where he did in Rosemount, County Westmeath, he didn't have any choice about playing football. The community there "eats, sleeps, and breathes GAA. It's a religion."

Gaelic football is a true community sport in Westmeath, involving friends, family and the entire community, which helped Boidu to fall in love with it as a child. He was lucky to have a coach at school who recognised his ability and took extra time to foster his talents.

Gaelic football, hurling, camogie, rounders and handball are the sports of the **GAELIC ATHLETIC ASSOCIATION** (GAA). The GAA is found all over the island of Ireland, and there are GAA teams outside Ireland in places like London and New York, where there are a lot of Irish immigrants.

Boidu is not your average GAA star. He is originally from Monrovia in Liberia and arrived in Ireland on his 8th birthday. He grew up in Liberia during the First Liberian Civil War. The only memories he has of the country are of gunshots, war and having to constantly move from place to place in search of shelter. It was not an environment that any child should have to grow up in.

From the minute he landed in Ireland to live with his adoptive parents, Boidu was excited, but he says that he was still a "scared little kid". Recalling his first days in his new school, he remembers thinking that everyone spoke differently, acted differently and even greeted each other differently than he was used to. He also remembers finding himself in a room filled only with White people for the first time in

The **FIRST LIBERIAN CIVIL WAR** began in 1989 and lasted until 1997 and was one of the bloodiest civil conflicts in recent African history.

his life and realising that his life would be very different from that point forward.

He arrived at his new school midway through the school year, a kid from a foreign country with a different accent, different colour skin and differently textured hair. But despite all of these differences, the other children welcomed him and treated him the same way they treated everyone else.

However, Boidu's experiences of childhood in Ireland weren't always perfect. On one occasion two boys told him that he didn't belong in Ireland and that he should "go back to where he came from". Boidu got upset, thinking that he didn't want to go back to where he came from because of how difficult his life had been prior to arriving in Ireland. He told his teacher, who struggled to respond to the incident. Luckily, the parents of the other boys took the incident seriously. They spoke to their kids about the wrongness of what they had said and got them to apologise for their actions. For Boidu, this was a great example of people coming together to have a real conversation about something that happened, and how kindness, understanding and a bit of education can help us understand how our actions impact others, and how to make up for mistakes we have made.

Boidu thinks it would be great if kids could learn about racism in school so that they could go home to their parents and teach them what they learned. This would help to create space for these conversations in Irish society. Young people can teach their parents about how Ireland is changing and help shape the views of their parents, who grew up in an Ireland that looked different to how it does today.

Boidu's GAA journey began in primary school, but it was the community spirit within the sport that kept him playing, improving and moving through the system, all the way up the ranks from his local team to the inter-county senior Westmeath team. Despite the overall positive experience of playing football, he has also experienced unfortunate side-effects of being one of the only Black people playing the sport at a high level. Standing out from the crowd because of the colour of his skin draws

Lara Dahunsi

Antrim footballer Lara Dahunsi, whose father moved to Ireland from Nigeria, was named Ulster's Young Player of the Year when she was 16.

Lara has been open about the difficulties she has faced in sport because of racism. Lara has experienced racist comments on and off the pitch, but she tries to focus on being the best player she can be at all times.

Lara would like to see the GAA, LGFA (Ladies' Gaelic Football Association) and Camogie Association acknowledge the difficulties that people of colour face when playing Gaelic sports. She wants to see the organisations support players of all backgrounds by ensuring everyone is treated with dignity and respect. She is dedicated to continuing to play the sport that she loves and to raising awareness about the issues she's faced so that other Black players don't have to go through what she's gone through.

Despite the challenges, Lara has had some amazing highlights as well, such as being named the TG4 Player of the Match for her spectacular effort during the All-Ireland Junior Ladies' Football Championship final at Croke Park in 2022.

attention to him, and when playing against other teams he has encountered racism from spectators not used to seeing Black people play GAA. "Sly comments" from fans and other players made Boidu question whether or not he belonged on the pitch. It was the support from his local team in Westmeath that reminded him that he did belong, that he was wanted and that he could become one of the best players in the sport.

Boidu is driven to constantly improve and be better than those that came before him. He even sees his own past self as competition and is always striving to be "better than he was yesterday". He knows that if it wasn't for the support of those who push him to achieve the absolute best, he wouldn't be where he is today. Boidu's coaches and fellow players, and even a competitive cousin, are all reasons why he has continued to experience success. One of the most influential people in his life was his grandfather, a White Irish man who was so welcoming to Boidu when he became part of his family. He encouraged Boidu to play GAA. He was always quick with the criticism, but all while putting a positive spin on everything Boidu did.

Encouraging more kids from the Black Irish community to play GAA is really important to Boidu. He emphasises that the benefits of playing GAA aren't just limited to health and wellbeing, but also include making lifelong friendships and being part of a supportive community. It can also help with scholarships for third-level education and even finding employment opportunities later on in life. Boidu thinks that if more people were aware of all the benefits of being a part of the GAA then more members of minority communities would take up the sports. When people aren't familiar with Gaelic sports and don't have family links to it, they may not be aware of how amazing it can be for children. But Boidu believes it is up to the GAA to do more outreach with minority communities and invite them to participate, and let them know how much the GAA can do for them and how much they can do for the GAA.

Boidu is often asked about his life story, and he has made himself vulnerable in his honesty about his journey. But if hearing his story encourages other people like him to join the GAA, he is happy to continue sharing it. He hopes that he is inspiring the future generation of GAA players, who might look a lot different from the players the sport has traditionally seen. He believes that bringing more diversity into the GAA will only bring more love and kindness to Gaelic sports.

Beryl Ohas

LGBTQIA+ activist

"Join hands and do something big"

BERYL OHAS, better known as Ohas, has been an activist for 10 years. Ten years is a long time to be working on any social justice cause, and Ohas's work for LGBTQIA+ rights has spanned the globe, from her native Kenya all the way to Ireland. Today Ohas is a social media content creator, a journalist, a machine operator for a pharmaceutical company and a cultural mediator for the International Organisation for Migration through the United Nations. She is also an investigative journalist and recently graduated from the Migrant Leadership Academy through the Immigrant Council of Ireland.

The Immigrant Council of Ireland is an organisation which fights for the rights of migrants in Ireland. Their Migrant Leadership Academy teaches the skills of community organising and activism to immigrants.

Ohas has always known that she was destined to "speak up". As a child, she was shy, but as the years went on, she realised that she wanted to share everything. Her motivation was the idea that even when she's long gone, young people would come across her work, be able to relate to it and find inspiration to keep going. She never thought her work would reach as many people as it has, with almost 40 thousand followers on Instagram.

Ohas has been attacked and suffered abuse because of her work as an LGBTQIA+ activist. But she still has a thirst to change people's minds. She finds it so powerful when she is able to change people's perspectives simply by giving them space to share and listen to each other's stories.

Born in Kenya, Ohas was raised by her grandparents. She had everything she needed growing up, but she realised in later years that not having her biological parents in her life meant there was something missing. But she is still grateful for the life that her grandparents gave her.

She came to Ireland in 2019, despite being told by the Irish she met in Kenya that she would need "a million umbrellas" when she got there. She sees a lot of similarities between Kenyan and Irish culture, and she has met a lot of good people in Ireland that have made her feel the "warmness of home".

Ohas researched Ireland quite a bit before deciding to move, but the most important thing for her was to get a sense of Black excellence in Ireland. She knew she was moving to a White-dominated country and she wanted to see how Black people in Ireland were faring in the face of racism and whether they were able to access services and resources. She found that when she arrived she was immediately directed to the right places to get the assistance she needed to be granted refugee status.

When an asylum seeker in Ireland is granted refugee status, they are entitled to remain in Ireland under the protection of the Irish state. This is the difference between an asylum seeker and a refugee.

Ohas's activism is about highlighting the problems that we *all* create. She believes that we are all capable of doing bad things or mistreating people, and that once we recognise this, we see that we have room for growth and making things better for everyone together. Ohas brings attention to these issues by speaking at social justice marches, like the Ireland For All March in February 2023, by sharing her story and by writing articles that are published by major news publications in Ireland.

By highlighting these issues Ohas helps to bring communities together to prevent future difficulties for everyone. Ohas finds happiness and a sense of safety in knowing that by helping to change the perspectives of others, she is creating a safer space for other members of the Black LGBTQIA+ community in Ireland.

As a member of the LGBTQIA+ community, Ohas has found that Ireland is much safer than the environment in Kenya. Nonetheless, what she finds to be one of the biggest differences between the LGBTQIA+ community in Ireland compared to Kenya is the lack of support she experiences when difficult circumstances arise. In Kenya she had a community that she could rely on to physically show up when homophobic attacks occurred, and there was comfort in knowing who she could rely on, no matter what.

In Kenya, sexual activity between people of the same sex is illegal and punishable by up to 14 years in prison.

Viola Gayvis

Viola Gayvis is a Black Dublin-based drag queen who is vocal not just about her support for LGBTQIA+ rights, but also about the rights of people of colour in Ireland. After the murder of George Floyd in 2020, Viola organised a digital drag event called "Ireland Cares" in aid of Black Pride Ireland.

Also known as Tafadzwa Donald Mzondo, Viola is well-known in the Irish drag art scene. She is only the second working Black drag queen in Ireland. She is open about her experiences as a "Drag Queen of Colour" and loves to talk about the power of challenging gender norms both as Viola and as her alter-ego, Donald.

Ohas says the LGBTQIA+ community in Ireland is both inclusive and exclusive at the same time. She has felt welcomed and included by some members of the LGBTQIA+ community from other minority groups, but there are always others who make her feel like she is not welcome in that space. She says there is division with the LGBTQIA+ community as much as within any other group of people. But she tries to focus on the positives and those members of the community who want to come together to work towards a stronger and safer space.

Ohas says that there is a lot of work to be done in the Black LGBTQIA+ community here in Ireland to create a safer space. She wants to see the community find ways to have fun and grow together while also lifting each other up. She wants the community to "join hands and do something big, or even if it's not big, just to be there for each other".

The Black LGBTQIA+ community has a lot to contend with in Ireland: having the Black and Irish identity along with being LGBTQIA+ is a lot for any person to deal with. Community is so important. Community is where you can find others who relate to you and understand your struggles. It's all about putting differences aside and lifting each other up. Ohas hopes that young people today will understand that supporting others involves more than just liking or resharing a post on social media. Real support requires showing up in person when someone is in need.

Gavin Bazunu

Ireland's number 1

"Pursue your passion"

GAVIN BAZUNU had two ambitions: to play for the Shamrock Rovers first team and to represent his country. He made his debut for Rovers in 2018 at the age of 16. Three years later he won his first cap for Ireland against Luxemburg.

Gavin was born in Dublin in 2002 to an Irish mother and a Nigerian father. While he has spent most of his life in Ireland, he is also very proud of being Nigerian. He has had the privilege of visiting his father's country on a number of occasions.

For Gavin, growing up in Ireland was amazing. He had a great group of friends and loved his time in school. Most importantly, he enjoyed playing football. Gavin's dad is a massive football fan and he got him involved in the sport from a young age.

Since Chris Hughton became the first Black Irish international footballer in 1979, Ireland fans have got used to seeing Black players in the green jersey. The current squad regularly features Black players such as Andrew Omobamidele and Adam Idah of Norwich City; Burnley's Michael Obafemi; and Chiedozie Ogbene of Luton Town.

Gavin reckons he played every outfield position before becoming a goalkeeper around the age of 13 or 14, and he hasn't looked back since. He began playing football for his school and also got involved with Shamrock Rovers at underage level. His dream of playing for the Shamrock Rovers first team was fuel for him to become the best player he could be, and before long he made it.

After making the Rovers first team in his teens, he was bought by one of the biggest clubs in the world, Manchester City, in 2019, on a 5-year contract. He made his debut for Manchester City's under-18s against Stoke City under-18s.

Man City sent Gavin out on loan to get more experience of first-team action. He played for Rochdale in League 1, keeping a clean sheet on his debut, a 1–0 victory against Huddersfield. The next season he moved to the south of England on loan to Portsmouth. At Portsmouth he was a popular character in the squad and at the end of a great season he was voted the 2020–21

Rianna Jarrett

Rianna Jarrett is an Irish–Jamaican footballer from Wexford. Her mother and father met in the UK and returned to Ireland where they had Rianna and her twin, Jordan. Rianna was a talented footballer from a young age and played with boys' teams until she reached the age where she could no longer play with them. She went to play for a local girls' club but was also picked for the Wexford select team that would play in the FAI Women's Cup.

Rianna received a sports scholarship to the University of Tennessee and set a new scoring record for the college. She also received the Offensive Player of the Year award there. Rianna has since had spells playing for Brighton and Hove Albion as well as the London City Lionesses before returning to her home club of Wexford Youths.

Rianna has been capped for Ireland since a young age and was part of the impressive under-17s team that had a lot of success. She currently has 16 caps for the senior team. She won her first cap against Italy in 2016 and has one goal for Ireland, scored in a win against Ukraine. Rianna was named FAI Women's Player of the Year in 2019.

Players' Player of the Season. He also won the overall League One Player of the Season award.

In March 2023 Ireland's under-15s put out a team against Latvia which had a majority of Black players! This shows the strength of the game among the Black Irish community and we can hope to see more Black players making it into the senior team in years to come.

After his award-winning season in League One, interest in Gavin was high among bigger clubs. In 2022 he made a permanent move to Premier League side Southampton. He went straight into the first team and got his first Premier League clean sheet in a 1–0 win over Bournemouth.

Gavin feels lucky to have not faced any discrimination while playing football, and that his skin colour didn't hold him back. Though racism does occur in football, Gavin feels that it has become a much more inclusive environment than it used to be.

Darren Randolph is a Mixed-Race goalkeeper who plays for AFC Bournemouth and has won 50 senior caps for Ireland. He started all of Ireland's matches at the European Championships in 2016. Darren's dad was a college basketball star in the US and he moved to Ireland as one of the first American imports into the Irish Basketball League.

One of Gavin's biggest inspirations as he was developing his game was Darren Randolph. It was important for him to see someone playing for Ireland with the same skin colour as him. For Darren to be playing in the same position as Gavin was a massive inspiration for him.

The proudest moments of Gavin's career so far have been his debuts for Rovers and for his country. Making his first appearance for Ireland was exhilarating for him. Unfortunately, he made his Ireland debut during the height of the COVID-19 pandemic so there weren't any fans in the stadium to cheer him on, but he knows many people around the country watched him play on TV. For Gavin, representing his nation is a special feeling and every time he puts on the jersey it still has that same meaning.

Gavin's advice to young players would be "all of the cliches that you hear about pursuing your passion" – because those are all the things that actually make the difference. Be dedicated, always show up on time and do the right things. Look after yourself and watch as much of the sport as you can.

Sky Sports pundit Clinton Morrison was born in London and made 36 appearances for Ireland, scoring 9 goals. He was part of the last Ireland squad to play at a World Cup in 2002.

But for Gavin, the most important message is: enjoy yourself. Learn to love the game. There are so many lows as well as highs in football as in life, and if you don't enjoy the game when the low times come, you won't stick with it. For Gavin, stepping out on the pitch is his happy place. He feels like he becomes untouchable on the pitch.

Emma Dabiri

Writer and historian

"Don't touch my hair"

EMMA DABIRI has a lot to say about hair. Specifically, she has a lot to say about Afro-textured hair, and what it can teach us about history, racism and the celebration of Blackness around the world. Emma is a historian, author and TV presenter currently living in London, but forever tied to her childhood in Ireland.

Emma's mother was born in Trinidad to Irish parents and her father was Nigerian. Emma was born in Dublin and during her early childhood her family spent some time in Atlanta, Georgia, a predominantly Black part of the United States. When her family moved back to Ireland she says it was "like going from colour to black-and-white". She really struggled with being one of the only Black people around. Growing up in the Rialto area of Dublin in the 1980s, she was constantly reminded of her difference, from other kids touching her hair without asking to being stared at in the playground. It was in Ireland that she heard the "n-word" for the first time.

Emma's dad actually spent some of his childhood in Ireland while Emma's grandfather was studying there. There was a community of Nigerian students in Dublin in the 1940s and 50s, but most of them returned home after the completion of their studies. Emma's father decided to return to Ireland to go to university, which is how her parents met.

It wasn't just that Emma stuck out in Dublin because of her skin colour. She struggled to care for her hair without having access to the speciality hair products which are readily available in the US for people with Afro hair. In America, Emma's hair had been kept in a neat Afro. When she moved to Ireland, her ability to care for her hair changed drastically. Remember, this was a time before you could buy things on the internet! Emma's mother did the best that she could, but after living in a place surrounded by other Black people, Emma knew that something was missing.

So Emma grew up with one White parent and one Black parent, but she was simply considered Black by most Irish people. When people would see her out with her mother they were shocked that she was White. Emma's Irishness was always questioned. When people asked her where she was "really" from they couldn't accept it when she answered that she was from Dublin. In fact, she would often make up different answers and say she was from places like Haiti or the Dominican Republic – which she would say in her Dublin accent – which people found more believable than when she said she was Irish.

Emma took an interest in history and racial injustice from a young age. In an act of defiance, she opted out of religious studies in her Catholic primary school and instead wrote an essay on the history of the transatlantic slave trade. Emma looks back on this as the first time she chose to do something that interested her instead of what others thought she should do.

Emma's first book, *Don't Touch My Hair*, was inspired by her experiences of trying to take care of her own hair without having access to the products and services her hair texture required. Emma remembers other little Irish girls around her having flowy long hair and desperately wanting hers to look like that. Emma's hair was not considered beautiful or feminine, which had a negative effect on how she viewed herself. She felt like her hair

From the 16th to the 19th century, slave traders transported enslaved people from Africa to North and South America. This is known as the **TRANSATLANTIC SLAVE TRADE**.

was a "problem" and that there was something "wrong" with her that needed to be fixed, even though her hair was just as beautiful as the next person's.

Emma's research into colonialism and African history taught her how important hair is within African cultures. For hundreds of years, African hair has been misunderstood and Black people have been taught that their hair is less than ideal because it is

Kit de Waal

Born Mandy Theresa O'Loughlin, Kit de Waal grew up in Birmingham, England, with her White Irish mother and Afro-Caribbean father. Growing up, she recalls being the only Black family at Irish social events, and the only Irish family in Afro-Carribean contexts.

Kit is an award-winning author of novels. Her first book, *My Name Is Leon*, focusses on the story of a Mixed-Race child growing up in the foster-care system, a world Kit knew well through her own work in criminal and family law in England. After the success of that novel, Kit was able to set up a fellowship to help disadvantaged writers pursue careers in creative writing.

Kit has published a memoir called *Without Warning and Only Sometimes: Scenes from an Unpredictable Childhood*, which details her life growing up in the 1970s with her mother, who was a Jehovah's Witness. Having two parents coming from two very different backgrounds meant that Kit was constantly at odds with two different belief systems, and she was often caught in between the two.

so different from White people's hair. For generations, Black people have chemically treated their hair to make it appear more like White hair, doing much damage to their natural hair in the process.

During the transatlantic slave trade, White people told stories about how Black people were inferior, in order to justify forcing African people into slavery. Generations of people all over the world were taught to believe that everything about Blackness was inferior to Whiteness. One of the messages people were told about Black hair was that it was like wool that grows on a sheep — which made Black people more like livestock than human beings. The stigma that surrounds Black hair today has its origins in these racist ideas from the colonial period.

Emma explains in her book that there are many ways that Black people can care for their hair while also displaying their culture, for example using protective hairstyles like cornrows, twists, Bantu knots and box braids. In fact, Emma has discovered that some of these hairstyles were once used as maps to help enslaved people escape to

A natural hair movement has been taking place globally over the past few years, with organisations like the C.R.O.W.N. (Creating a Respectful and Open World for Natural Hair) Coalition in the US and the Halo Collective in the UK (of which Emma is an ambassador). By increasing awareness about positive aspects of wearing natural hairstyles, these movements are working to improve the lives of Black men and women all over the world.

Britain's first colony was their closest neighbour to the west: Ireland. Some of the same strategies of dehumanisation that were used towards African people were also used to make the Irish seem less than fully human.

freedom! The complexity of some ancient styles of braids and cornrows shows just how sophisticated the civilisations that existed in Africa were.

Emma can remember the first time she saw her type of hair texture in a TV show or movie: in 2014, when she was already an adult. She's so glad that young Black people today are able to see natural hair represented in media and entertainment. And she's delighted to see more Black people wearing their hair naturally in recent years, instead of chemically straightening and damaging it. She could never have imagined the representation of natural hair that's visible around the world now.

CORNROWS are made by separating hair into sections and then braiding it from the scalp into different shapes towards the back of the head. Braiding and twisting Afro-textured hair helps to protect the hair by keeping the ends free from damage by not allowing them to get dry.

Emma's second book is *What White People Can Do Next: From Allyship to Coalition*. It's about how White people can work with Black people to change the racism in society. Emma believes that people of all backgrounds need to come together to create real change. She believes that change is possible in Ireland, and because the country is diversifying so quickly, *now* is the time for Irish people to make sure that everyone is represented and treated equally.

Emma's relationship with Ireland has always been difficult. She was subjected to so much racism in Dublin that she moved to London as soon as she could when she turned 18. More recently, however, Emma has begun to rekindle her relationship with her homeland and has even started brushing up on her Irish-language skills to strengthen her ties to her Irish roots. Growing up Emma never understood why people told her she was "half" Irish. For her, there is more than one way to "be Irish".

Emma is glad to see more diversity in Ireland now and is encouraged by the formation of the Black Irish identity. She hopes that anyone who finds that idea difficult will understand that adding something new to Irish identity doesn't mean taking anything away from their idea of Irishness. She is also relieved to see an appetite for change among Irish people.

Emma hopes that future generations of Black Irish people are no longer subjected to questions about their identity or asked the infamous question: "Where are you *really* from?" She hopes that they will be accepted by everyone as part of the fabric of Irish society.

Dr Phil Mullen

Black Studies lecturer at Trinity College Dublin

"Empowering the Black mind in Ireland"

PHIL MULLEN is an activist with the Association of Mixed Race Irish and a lecturer in Black Studies at Trinity College in Dublin. Having grown up in institutions in Ireland, Phil overcame a lot of obstacles to get to where she is today, and she has done a lot to help others who have faced the same challenges in their lives.

The **CELTIC TIGER** was the name given to an explosion of economic activity and wealth in Ireland in the 1990s. Prior to the Celtic Tiger, there was very little immigration into Ireland. Ireland was a land of emigration, with large numbers of young people going abroad in search of opportunities. Since the 1990s, Ireland has begun attracting immigrants in much larger numbers.

Phil was born in Dublin. Her mother was Irish and her father was Nigerian. They met in Belfast while her father was on a fellowship at Queen's University. Phil's mother returned to Dublin, and after Phil was born she was placed in an institution for "illegitimate" children in Galway and later moved to another institution in Dublin. Her mother would come to the institution once a week and bring a group of girls out so as not to raise suspicions about her connection to Phil. Phil's father was involved in her life too but he had a family back in Nigeria that took more of his attention.

Phil moved in with her mother after she left the institution at the age of 16. Phil describes herself as a "pre-Celtic Tiger" Black Irish person: someone who was in Ireland while there were still few Black people living here.

Despite knowing who her parents were and moving in with her mother while she was still at school, Phil struggled to adjust to life outside of institutions. She ended up dropping out of school. She worked a number of low-paying jobs, including as a chambermaid, a kitchen porter and a cleaner. While working as a cleaner in RTÉ, Ireland's state TV and radio broadcaster, she remembers feeling invisible. She would walk into a room where people were talking and they wouldn't even notice she was there. This lit a spark in Phil. She decided she was going to return to education and change her life.

For 12 years Phil worked with the **IRISH TRAVELLER MOVEMENT**. She loved the sense of social justice in that job, and was inspired by how members of the Travelling community were so passionate about justice and fighting the discrimination they faced in Ireland.

Phil went back and finished secondary school, and went on to study English and philosophy at Trinity College Dublin. She then started a master's degree, but she dropped out halfway through it. She longed to emigrate as she hated Ireland at that point of her life. She hated how White people had treated her because of her skin colour, and she wanted to live in a more diverse place. She eventually moved to London but she came back to Ireland, and then found herself falling back into the cycle of low-paying work. Phil once again made the decision to go back and finish what she had started. She finished her master's, and went on to do a PhD looking at how Black Irish women like herself who grew up in the Irish institutional system thought about their identity.

In the 1990s, a lot of stories began coming out in Ireland about abuse that happened in institutions like industrial schools and Mother-and-Baby Homes. Phil was pleased to see these stories being told, but she was worried that little focus was put on the discrimination faced by Black and Mixed-Race children in those institutions. In her work with the Association of Mixed Race

Irish, Phil has helped shine a light on the experiences of children like her in Irish institutions.

Phil's advice for young people who want to become university teachers and researchers is to have a long-term goal and work towards it. Have a picture in your mind of what you would like to do or who you would like to be after you complete your degree. Phil also believes in the power of building networks and getting to know all the people and services that can support you and that you can learn from along the way.

Phil is concerned by the low number of Black students who are doing postgraduate degrees in Ireland. She would love to

Louie Lyons

Phil Mullen's son Louie is an aspiring academic, studying Middle Eastern, Jewish and Islamic civilisations and Classics at Trinity College Dublin. Trinity is where he began his first project – the renaming of the Berkeley Library.

This library on the grounds of Trinity College had been named after the Irish philosopher George Berkeley in 1978. George Berkeley was a slaveowner who also defended slavery in his writing, so the naming of the library after him was considered highly problematic.

Louie was instrumental in organising a movement among the students of Trinity to have Berkeley's name removed from the library. Following that success, Louie hopes to continue working in the field of decolonisation, in particular looking at the lack of racially conscious history teaching in Irish schools.

see more people from the Black and Mixed-Race community furthering their education. She believes that by ensuring they link in with as many aspects of campus life as possible, Black students will begin to see more opportunities for themselves and feel encouraged to continue their university educations.

Phil wants to see the Black and Mixed-Race communities in Ireland continue to build a strong sense of self. She believes we have a lot of work to do to make sure that people who come to live in Ireland are made to feel safe and welcome. Her focus is on getting Ireland to have a good conversation about immigration and asylum seekers, without the discussion becoming too polarised or descending into chaos. She believes a lot of that will depend on housing, as we need to have enough places for migrants to live.

Phil hopes to see more Black people break the moulds that society puts them in and begin to challenge the status quo. She wants to see the "Black mind" empowered in Ireland.

Monjola

Musical artist

"You really got to love yourself"

MONJOLA'S RISE IN the Irish music scene has been meteoric. Just two years passed between releasing his first song during the COVID-19 pandemic to going on a European tour with the American rapper Kid Cudi. He has flourished on stages from Dublin to Amsterdam, Paris to Milan. Monjola knows how to pull a team together too. He co-founded the Chamomile Records group alongside fellow Black Irish artists Aby Coulibaly and Moyo, and together they run amazing music events around the country. The sky's the limit for Monjola and Chamomile.

Monjola is a Nigerian-Irish artist from Dublin. He was born in Lagos, Nigeria, and moved to Ireland when he was four years old. He describes growing up in Ireland as an interesting experience. At times he struggled with his Black and Irish identity and had an "identity crisis" when he was young. This was tough for Monjola, but he got through it by knowing himself and what he wanted to do.

Having an **IDENTITY CRISIS** is a common experience in young people who have multiple ethnicities or nationalities. Living with one culture at home while experiencing a different culture outside can lead to feeling like you are living two different lives and having to "**CODE SWITCH**". This is when you talk, think and act differently in one place than another.

Monjola comes from a creative family with a brother who also creates music and a sister who is a spoken-word poet. The siblings grew up around music. Monjola feels like music found him and it was natural for him to get into making it.

Mojola is inspired by international artists like Pharrell Williams and Labyrinth. He was also motivated by Irish artists who were succeeding. He cites the likes of Black Irish rapper Rejjie Snow as inspirations. When he saw other Irish artists thriving, that gave him a push to succeed as well.

Monjola's debut single was 2020's "Know You". This catchy song blends Monjola's skills in rapping and singing. He followed it with "Feels Right" later that year, which showcased his ability to write upbeat and catchy music. In 2021 Monjola released three more songs: "Smile", "Where U At", which features Monjola's Chamomile collaborator Aby Coulibaly, and "Pain Don't Die". "Smile", one of his most critically acclaimed songs, has 2 million streams on Spotify. With "Pain Don't Die", Monjola demonstrated his musical range as well as his ability to bring more emotional depth to his work.

He carried on releasing music in 2022 with "Extrovert", "Big Fat Liar" and "Mama Always Says". These songs brought a whole new wave of supporters and allowed Monjola to reach for new opportunities. In November 2022, he had the opportunity to travel and tour with American hip-hop icon Kid Cudi. Monjola knew he couldn't let this opportunity pass, and he put on incredible performances in major European cities. His fanbase exploded after this and it taught Monjola just how far music can travel.

Monjola has been contributing a lot to the creative scene in Ireland, particularly the Black Irish creative scene which is growing larger and larger every day. He recently built his own studio in Dublin which allows him to give other creatives opportunities to make their art.

Monjola's big hope for Ireland is that there will be more affordable housing and more creative spaces so that young people don't feel like they have to leave. He really hopes that the art and music scene here continues to grow and gets more appreciation from outside Ireland.

Black Irish musicians

There are so many Black Irish musicians making waves in the Irish scene today. Here are just a few to look out for, but there are lots more.

Denise Chaila

Denise is the star of any room she walks into! She has performed as Ed Sheeran's support act and appeared at festivals across Ireland and Europe. This Zambian-Irish singer and rapper moved to Ireland at the age of three. Denise began her music career in 2012 as part of a budding music scene in Limerick alongside artists like GodKnows, Murli and the Rusangano family. Denise released her first EP in 2019, titled *Dual Citizenship*, followed in 2020 by her first album, *Go Bravely*, which features beloved tracks like "Anseo" and "Chaila". It won the Choice Music Award for Album of the Year in 2020. Denise cofounded Narolane Records, which has contributed so much to the Limerick and Irish music scenes.

Jazzy

Yasmine Byrne, known professionally as Jazzy, is an Irish pop-dance singer-songwriter who became the first Irish woman to reach number 1 on the Spotify charts. As part of the group Belters Only, Jazzy has hit the UK singles charts with "Make Me Feel Good" and "Don't Stop Just Yet", while her solo single "Giving Me" reached number 3 in the UK.

TraviS and Elzzz

Dublin-based rap duo TraviS and Elzzz made history recently by becoming the highest-charting rappers ever from Ireland, reaching number 2 in the Irish charts with their album *Full Circle*. The pair are also part of the group Gliders which has seen massive success with their clothing and events brands.

Aby Coulibaly

Co-founder with Monjola and Moyo of Chamomile Records, Aby is a soulful R&B singer-songwriter from Dublin. Her father is from Senegal and her mother is from Ireland. Aby's songs have a timeless feel and feature her ability to flawlessly transition between singing and rapping. Her 2020 debut single "Taurus" has over 1.8 million streams.

Tolü Makay

Tolü, born in Nigeria and raised in Ireland, emerged onto the Irish music scene in 2018 with her debut single "Goodbye", which currently has more than 1 million streams. She has a soulful sound with influences ranging from Erykah Badu to Amy Winehouse. Since the start of her career she has sold out shows in many towns across Ireland and performed on national TV.

Selló

Selló is a rapper from Dublin who has been making waves with his sound. Selló created history in 2022 with the first drill tape to chart in the top 10 in Ireland. The album peaked at 6 in the charts.

JyellowL

Jean-Luc Adenrele Ibraham Koko Uddoh, known by his stage name JyellowL, is a popular Irish rapper of Nigerian and Afro-Jamaican descent. He made his music debut in 2016 and has gone on to perform at Longitude, had his music featured in the FIFA 20 video game and performed at the 3Arena.

The people behind the music

There are many Black Irish people involved in the Irish music scene off-stage, helping musicians to create. Sound engineer Tunde Esho, also known as Mixed by Simba, has been listed as one of the top 10 producers in Ireland by *District* magazine. He is the owner of Jungle Beam Studio. His colleague Joel Safo is a Drogheda-raised entrepreneur. Safo is the head of A&R at Trust It Entertainment as well as a manager for many different artists in Ireland. We are also seeing a burst of Black-owned organisations helping to promote music in Ireland and around the world. Vision Lab is a photography and videography studio that has helped many Irish artists and creatives start their careers. The likes of Slight Motif and other promotional organisations are also crucial in getting Black Irish artists' work more widely recognised.

Ola Majekodunmi

Irish-language media star

"Once you embrace who you are, it's freedom"

WHEN OLA MAJEKODUNMI'S parents moved to Ireland from Nigeria with their 7-month-old baby daughter, they couldn't have imagined that she'd grow up to be one of the most prominent *gaeilgeoirí* – fluent Irish speakers – in the country. But they sent her to the local Irish-speaking *gaelscoil* and she has gone on to become the first person of African descent to be appointed to the board of Foras na Gaeilge, the organisation that is responsible for Irish-language policy on the island of Ireland.

Learning Irish was never a problem for Ola, but the fact that she wasn't White and was attending an Irish-language school was sometimes a problem for others. A prominent anti-immigrant campaigner used to actually wait near her school to harass Ola's parents and the parents of other non-White students, asking why their children were allowed to attend an Irish-language school. The principal of her school faced criticism after appearing on the Irish-language TV station TG4 to talk about celebrating diversity in an Irish-language school. It seemed that there were some people who just couldn't understand why the Irish language should be shared with people who weren't ethnically Irish.

GAELSCOILEANNA are primary schools in Ireland that operate exclusively through the Irish language. They are popular with Irish parents as well as immigrants.

Ola's secondary school was less diverse than her primary school, and as one of the first non-White students in the school, Ola experienced some challenges. She often felt like students and teachers had difficulty figuring out how to communicate with her because she was different from the others. But Ola believes those problems were down to a lack of experience with people who were different, rather than racism. In fact that school has since become one of Ola's biggest supporters throughout her career.

From a young age Ola loved performing and being on stage, and her parents remember her as a little girl walking up to strangers in a hotel and pretending to interview them. Her parents encouraged her creativity by enrolling her in the famous Billie Barry Stage School, which helped Ola to find her voice and be her true self. Later, in Transition Year, she did work experience in media through Gael Linn, which taught her the fundamentals of filmmaking and radio production. It was then that she began working with Raidió na Life, the Irish-language radio station where she still works today.

GAEL LINN is an organisation which promotes the Irish language, particularly through the arts. Gael Linn produces media and runs a record label that releases music sung in Irish.

RAIDIÓ NA LIFE is a Dublin-based Irish-language radio station broadcasting online and on 106.4 FM.

It wasn't until Ola was doing her degree in English, media and cultural studies at Dún Laoghaire Institute of Art, Design and Technology (IADT) that she finally had a chance to talk about Blackness and her racial identity. College was the first environment where Ola felt comfortable speaking openly about her experiences as a Black Irish woman.

Ola went on to do a master's degree in digital broadcast production at IADT. As part of her coursework, she wanted to design a studio production that focused on Black identity, but struggled to find guidance from her teachers on how to set up lighting for people with darker skin. Because of how lighting on film sets works, different skin tones need different coloured lights to help them look their best. Despite being the only Black student on her course, Ola felt confident and empowered to bring the issue up with her lecturers as a point for further discussion.

Ola has been in the media industry since 2014, working on productions with RTÉ, TG4 and the BBC. She has done a lot of radio and TV work, along with speaking at events and on panels, usually about the importance of discussing identity and the Irish language. Ola's radio work includes her long-running programme on Raidió na Life called *Afra-Éire*, about African-Irish music and

Zainab Boladale

Zainab Boladale was the first person of African descent to work in the RTÉ newsroom when she became one of the presenters of the children's programme *news2day* in 2017. Originally from Nigeria, Zainab moved to Ennis, County Clare, when she was 4 years old.

After she started working on TV, Zainab faced a lot of racist abuse online. Thankfully, RTÉ called out the negativity. This led to a YouTube channel that was targeting Zainab being taken down. Zainab has openly spoken about her experiences of racism both online and offline, including negative comments she has received while filming the programme *Nationwide* all over the country.

Zainab doesn't let the negative comments get in the way of her doing the job she loves. She hopes that by speaking out about her experiences she can help put a stop to this form of racism, so that future Black Irish journalists don't have to go through the same things that she has.

culture. She was one of the first broadcasters to highlight African-Irish artists like Tolü Makay. Ola finds Raidió na Life to be one of the best radio stations in Ireland in terms of embracing the diversity of the island.

One of Ola's most well-known productions is a video that she made in 2018 called "What Does Irishness Look Like?", which features young people from a variety of backgrounds speaking Irish and discussing their experiences growing up in Ireland. This was one of the first videos featuring the diversity of modern Ireland, and Ola is so happy that it sparked conversation about this important topic. The video currently has over 46,000 views on YouTube.

While Ola initially wanted to bring attention to the difficulties people of colour in Ireland were facing by creating unique media content, she now hopes to move away from just talking about Blackness and racism in Ireland. She's passionate about bringing attention to the Irish language for young people in Ireland and is currently involved in making new TV shows in Irish. She acknowledges that the media industry is a tough one to be in, and her Blackness can often make it more difficult, but she loves her work and will continue to pave the way for other young people to follow in her footsteps.

Ola isn't just passionate about the Irish language, she also loves the Yoruba language, which is one the many languages spoken in Nigeria. She is interested in exploring the shared history of the two languages and even the shared colonial history of Ireland and Nigeria. She feels that there are so many links between the two cultures and that it's important for us to learn about them in order to understand each other.

Ola wants young Black Irish people to feel proud of their identities and to see how many amazing things have been coming from their community in recent years. "Be proud of who you are," she says, "don't try too hard to fit in." When she was younger she remembers feeling like she needed to change her appearance to fit in with those around her, but she says, "Once you embrace who you are, it's just beautiful. It's just freedom." She acknowledges that there will always be some sort of struggle with racism because human beings have difficulty accepting others for who they are, but at the end of the day there is always love, and there always going to be people out there who will support you.

More than 54 million people speak the YORUBA language, most of them in Nigeria, with many also in Benin and Togo. It is the language of the Yoruba ethnic group. There are over 500 languages spoken in Nigeria. English is Nigeria's official, and most widely spoken, language.

Ola's hope for Ireland is for people to truly accept the country's beautiful diversity and know that people from different communities are not here to take anything away from Irish culture, but to add to it. She wants young people who feel different to trust that it does get better, that they are not alone, and to keep going. She also hopes that the Black and Irish community will embrace the Irish language more as part of their identity. In fact, she is responsible for literally changing the language by introducing a new term for "person of colour": *duine de dhath.* How amazing is that?!

Manni the Barber

Afro hair specialist

"Building up the next generation of Black Irish barbers"

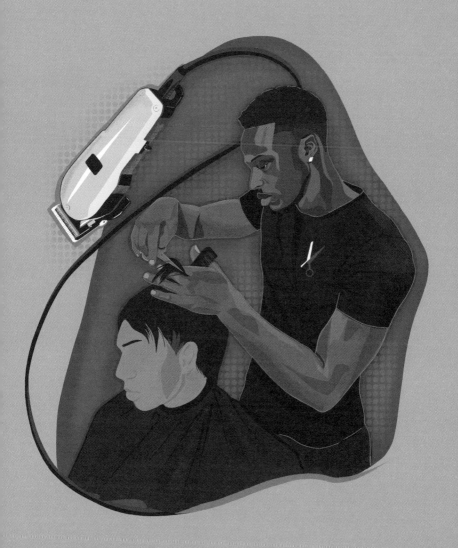

MANNI FIRST STARTED cutting hair when he was 16 as a side hobby in his mother's kitchen, with his mates as his regular customers. He saw barbering as an artform and a passion – he didn't think he could really make money from it. But there turned out to be a real market for someone who could cut Afro hair. He used to think 5 customers was a busy day, and now he owns two barbershops!

As his business grew, Manni's parents moved the barbershop out of the kitchen and into the family shed. He invested the profits he made from cutting hair into kitting out the shed with wallpaper, a couch and a TV. Manni's barbershop quickly became a social hub for the lads in the neighbourhood, with boys popping over for chats even when they didn't need a haircut.

Emmanuel Mawoyeka, also known as Manni, came to Ireland from Nigeria when he was two years old with his parents and 4 siblings, first living in Dublin and then settling in Navan, County Meath. He recalls everyone being friendly and welcoming during his childhood, despite being in the minority as a Black family in early 2000s Ireland. Manni is happy that he grew up in Ireland as it suits his quiet personality. He's glad that he's been able to benefit from the safety and peace that Ireland gave him and his family.

Manni doesn't have strong memories of Nigeria. As he grew up immersed in the culture around him in Ireland, he didn't connect with his Nigerian identity until he was a teenager. It was then that he realised that he could embrace both sides of his identity – that he could really be both Black and Irish. He went to a relatively diverse secondary school in Navan where there were other Black students. However it was during this period that he first experienced racism and microaggressions. He was glad to have friends around him who understood his experiences when negative incidents happened, and that they were able to stick together so that they weren't on their own going through difficult things.

Manni was expected to go to college after school because his family placed a lot of emphasis on education. He studied business in the hope it would lead to a good career. He fell short on Leaving Cert points and wasn't able to go to his first choice university, but he was glad that some of his mates at school went with him to Dundalk Institute of Technology.

Manni didn't see himself cutting hair for a living, but after finding joy and success doing it through secondary school, he continued offering his skills when he went to college. Dundalk was a place that desperately needed Afro hair barbers, so the word quickly spread and he became very busy. He moved into student accommodation full-time during his final year of college, and that's when things really took off. Before he knew it, he even had parents bringing their kids to him and secondary school students showing up in his flat looking for haircuts.

MICROAGGRESSIONS are small, subtle or low-key comments or behaviours based on a person's race, gender, age, ability and so on. Sometimes they are intended as compliments by well-meaning people, but they make people feel uncomfortable and draw attention to how they don't fit in.

Dundalk IT is a very diverse college, with an African Society. Manni loved getting to meet other Black people and learn more about his culture through the society's programmes and events.

When Manni graduated during the COVID-19 lockdown in 2020, he decided to take the opportunity to devote his time to being a barber instead of getting a different job. It was something that he really enjoyed and he figured he could make a decent living from it. He took a year to just cut hair in his own home and see how things went.

LOCKDOWNS during the 2020–22 COVID-19 pandemic meant that schools, colleges, businesses and public places were shut for long periods to slow the spread of the dangerous virus.

That year confirmed for Manni that he was destined to be a barber. At the end of it he opened his first barbershop in Dundalk. It was instantly successful. Never one to settle, Manni decided to push himself out of his comfort zone again. He opened up a second shop, in Drogheda, another Irish town that was in desperate need of a barber who could cut Afro as well as other hair and offer a truly multicultural barbershop experience. Manni knows that there are many towns in Ireland that need services like this, and if he had all the resources and manpower in the world, he would be opening up shops all over the country – that is his plan anyway!

Now Manni is working hard to train other barbers to help him grow his business and achieve his dream of having a Black-owned barbershop in every Irish town. Manni believes that there is a huge gap in terms of education and training for cutting Afro hair in cosmetology courses in Ireland. He is dedicated to building up new barbers. He currently runs a part-time barber-development programme for aspiring barbers so that he can develop skills in the community. He has hired several graduates from this programme as staff in his shops. While it does help him grow his own business, he also just wants to help others to achieve their potential, even if some of them will go off on their own and start their own businesses.

Black Irish people are a unique minority that is growing quickly and Manni knows that they are only just getting started. He is so proud of how well the community is doing, given it is still new to the country. Manni has had a few experiences of being

Adizat Oseni

Nigerian-born businesswoman Adizat Oseni has known that there was a real need for a Black hair salon in Ireland ever since she started doing hair in her mother's kitchen back in 2013. She knows first-hand how difficult it is for Black women to get quality salon services in Ireland. She wants to provide Black women in Ireland with the professional salon experience that they deserve. HBA Studio in Smithfield, Dublin, has become the place to go for stylists who have an intricate knowledge of Afro hair.

No one should be turned away from a salon because of their hair type, but that's what happened to Adizat time and time again, which she says is a practice that really needs to be addressed in the industry. Adizat wants to be able to cater to everyone who walks through the doors of HBA, but she also wants other salons in Ireland to do the same. She wants care for Afro hair to be added to beauty and cosmetology course curriculums so that every salon can start catering to all hair types, rather than forcing Black women to find help in less professional settings or specialist salons.

overlooked for opportunities that were given to White people instead. He hopes to see the Black Irish community grow to the point where they are in positions to pick other people of colour for amazing opportunities.

Manni would love to see the day when you can walk around any town in Ireland and see Black-owned business all around you. He knows that there are loads of Black Irish people doing hair at home and he wants to encourage them to get out and open up their own shops so that others can benefit from the important service that they can offer. He hopes his shops will inspire others to do just that.

Mamobo Ogoro

Founder of GORM

"On a mission to unify the world"

HAVE YOU EVER had a conversation with someone you didn't agree with? Have you ever thought: *This person just doesn't understand me. How can I even talk to them?* These are the types of conversations that Mamobo Ogoro, founder of media company GORM, would like us all to have in order to change the world. With GORM, Mamobo is hoping to help people understand one another, which she feels is getting more and more difficult in this age of division.

Mamobo founded GORM after George Floyd's murder in 2020. She saw the world growing more and more polarised, or divided, and was finding it difficult to have conversations with people who had different opinions to herself. She wanted to create a space where differently minded people can meet in the middle and break down the barriers between them. She also wanted GORM to be a space where people belonging to ethnic and religious minority groups who weren't Black could be heard and understood. Mamobo is working on bringing her message of unity and understanding to everyone in Ireland through her workshops and speaking events and the digital content she produces.

When Mamobo Ogoro moved to Ireland from Lagos, Nigeria in the year 2000 with her single mother and siblings, she had no idea

---

Traditionally, the Irish for "Black person" is *duine gorm*. But *gorm* literally means blue! This is because in Irish you describe a White person with dark features (such as dark hair) as being *dubh*, which means "black".

Recently Black broadcaster and Irish-language advocate Ola Majekodunmi has suggested Irish speakers use the term *duine de dhath*, "person of colour", and this has been added to the official registry of Irish terms.

that she was any different to other three-year-olds. Despite being the first migrant family in their small council estate in Enniscorthy in County Wexford, it wasn't until she started school that the colour of her skin was used to separate her from her peers.

When she entered primary school, Mamobo was immediately placed in an English as an Additional Language class, despite English being her first language. When she was moved to a mainstream classroom, she remembers another girl asking her why her skin "looked like poo". It was this moment that she understood that she was different, and that society had decided that she belonged in the racial box of "Black". She knew even then, at the young age of 6, that this was not a label she chose, but something society gave her.

A strong-willed middle child whose nicknames in Pidgin English were *Jaga Jaga*, meaning "all over the place" or "uncontrollable", and *over-sabi*, meaning "know-it-all", Mamobo was never content to accept the negative treatment she experienced and saw around her. She was always curious and found herself wondering, *Why do people treat us differently? Why do people hate?* But she struggled to find the answers she needed from those around her. Mamobo grew up in a time when no one was really talking about injustice or questioning why things were the way they were, which was something she never understood.

PIDGIN ENGLISH

A "pidgin" is a mix of different languages. Pidgins form so that people from different ethnic groups can communicate using a shared language. English is the official language of Nigeria, but there are many other languages spoken there as well, and Pidgin English is often used in informal conversation.

Secondary school was also filled with negative experiences. Mamobo's first year at an all-girls school was one of the most toxic environments she has ever been in. It was only later that she looked back and realised that most of the bullying she experienced was due to her race. She and her sister were the only Black students in the school and Mamobo recalls being labelled a

Mick Abidoye

When a career-ending injury cut short Mick Abidoye's dreams of playing professional soccer, he could have easily let this life-changing event derail his hopes of success. Instead, Mick channelled his passion into a new career as an entrepreneur and creator of the social media platform Created in Éire (@createdineire on Instagram). Mick started the platform with the goal of sharing all of the amazing Irish talent in music, sports and business with the world. He especially wanted to highlight young people who are underrepresented in the entertainment industry.

Mick is inspired by the entrepreneurial spirit of his father, an accountant who owned his own firm, who passed away at the age of 46. Mick is driven to live up to his dad's legacy and not let anything stop him from achieving his dreams. He set up Created in Éire in 2020, in the midst of the COVID-19 pandemic. He went on to become the youngest recipient of an award at the inaugural Black and Irish Gala in 2021 and then again in 2022. He has since earned a degree in business from the Atlantic Institute of Technology, Sligo, and is ready for his next big business adventure!

thief and having monkey noises made behind her back. Eventually, she found her community with other "outcasts" in the mixed-sex school she moved to from 2nd year. Mamobo's circle of friends were not the "popular kids", but they were people who understood what it meant to be picked on because they were different.

Mamobo's natural inquisitiveness didn't fade as she got older. She kept wondering, *Why do people treat us differently?* and this led her to study psychology and criminal justice at the University of Limerick. She fell in love with social psychology, which is the study of human behaviour in social groups. This helped her understand what had been happening to her for her whole life.

When she finished her degree, Mamobo struggled to decide what to do next with her life. Throughout her teenage and early adult years, she was unable to find work because, she believes, people didn't want to hire someone with an African name, a type of racism that is also known as "name-based discrimination". Her mother suggested using her middle name, Naomi, but Mamobo felt her name was an important part of her identity. She loves to tell people that she is the only Mamobo on Google!

Mamobo identifies as **AFRO-IRISH** or **NIGERIAN-IRISH** because she wants to highlight her ethnic identity and not just see herself as Black. She says that there is more to her than just her Blackness, and it is important to her to distinguish her ethnic and cultural identity so that others will understand that all Black people do not fall into a single category, but rather have individual stories and experiences to share.

Mamobo's name literally translates to "the right hand of God" and she believes that she truly embodies her name by supporting and serving her community in the best way that she can.

With few other options at the time, Mamobo decided to continue on her academic journey and enrolled in a psychology master's programme at the University of Limerick. She focused her research on how ideas about racism affect Afro-Irish people and their sense of identity and belonging. She found that the older generation felt more "Irish" and the younger generation didn't connect with the Irish identity as strongly. For older people, physical things like Irish passports and driver's licences made them feel Irish, but younger people felt that "Irishness" was something *inside* a person. She also found that the younger generation of Afro-Irish people didn't identify as strongly with their African heritage because of misrepresentations of what it means to be "African" in Irish society (like the use of images of starving children for charity drives). These young people leaned in more to their racial identity and their Blackness, rather than feeling African, because of the negative associations with Africa.

At 21 years of age Mamobo was offered a fully-funded PhD programme at the University of Limerick, which she is working on now. Her research focuses on how ideas about identity affect people who were born in Ireland to parents who were born abroad ("second generation migrants"). She wants to explore how these people see their national and racial identity, and find out how much impact society and the media has on how they see themselves. This research is what ultimately helped her establish her company, GORM.

Mamobo defines GORM as "an intercultural media and communications company that is on a mission to unify across social, political and cultural differences in order to help people in marginalised communities feel like they belong". One of the main things GORM has produced so far is the This is "Them" project, which films people having conversations about being from marginalised groups, such as being disabled or a member of the LGBTQIA + community. The videos are shared online, with the goal of reaching as many people as possible.

In order to change a person's viewpoint about people who are not like them, the conversations need to be engaging and interesting and, ultimately, encourage us to think a little bit differently about other people.

Mamobo doesn't call GORM a "safe space", but a "safe-enough space" for difficult conversations.

Mamobo wants GORM to be a place where perspectives can be challenged, but always with human dignity and respect. People need to listen to each other, even if they don't agree. The goal of GORM is to be the place for those conversations to happen. Mamobo says that this work is not about changing minds, but about people being heard and respected as human beings, and having their identity respected. She wants to reshape the ideas that we have of different and diverse communities in Ireland. For example, Mamobo feels that discussions about Black people too often focus on sad stories.

She says that she is on a "personal mission to unify the world" and hopes to bring Ireland right along with her. Her dream is to live in an Ireland where "through the beauty of the differences and diversity that we have, we can see our humanity". She believes that your experiences and all the facets of your identity are part of your human experience but do not fully define who you are.

Mamobo dreams of a world where we can all be seen as people who have value and worth, and are not judged because of our religion or the colour of our skin.

Phil Lynott

Rock star

"The Ace with the Bass"

PHIL LYNOTT was a true rock star. He was the first Black Irishman to gain international attention and commercial success for his music. As the frontman of the legendary band Thin Lizzy, he created massive hits which still resonate today, such as "The Boys Are Back in Town" and "Dancing in the Moonlight". As well as writing the band's songs, Phil both sang lead vocals and played bass at the same time.

Phil was born in England in 1949 to an Irish mother and a Brazilian father. He was sent to Ireland to live with his grandparents while his mother remained in the UK. Years later, when Thin Lizzy were performing in London, he tried to find his dad, whom he had been told was a barber. He didn't find him and never knew him. Phil grew up in Crumlin, Dublin, as a lively and outgoing young kid. He began playing the guitar at 11 years of age.

"When I'm in England, I say I'm from Ireland. When I'm in Ireland, I say I'm from Dublin. When I'm in Dublin, I say I'm from Crumlin. When I'm in Crumlin, I say, Leighlin Road. When I'm in Leighlin Road, I say, I'm a Lynott." — Phil Lynott

Friends of Phil's when he was growing up recall him being racially abused in Dublin. When he started playing music, he also faced discrimination from the mainstream radio who didn't want to play his music due to the colour of his skin. But Phil did not allow prejudice to stop him from becoming the rock star he was meant to be. Later in life he would joke that being Black and Irish was "like being a pint of Guinness".

Phil played in a few bands before starting Thin Lizzy in 1969 with drummer Brian Downey and guitarist Eric Bell. The name came from a comics character called Tin Lizzy. They changed it to Thin Lizzy as a joke about the Dublin accent that pronounces the "th" as a "t". The band went through a lot of lineup changes over the years but Lynott and Downey, one of the great rock drummers, remained the core of the band as different guitar players came and went.

Thin Lizzy quicky won attention in Ireland for their high-energy performances. Key to their early success was the exotic figure of their larger-than-life frontman. At a time when there were few people of colour in Dublin, Phil Lynott, a tall Black man with an Afro hairstyle, who had a daring fashion sense and walked with a swagger, looked like a star in the making. On stage he brought huge energy and confidence to his performances. The band took the local Dublin rock scene by storm.

But commercial success, and recognition outside Ireland, was harder to come by. Phil Lynott's story is about perseverance and hard work as much as talent. Thin Lizzy had to wait for their third album to score their first hit single. Their hard-rock version of the old Irish folk song "Whiskey in the Jar" was a bold statement. It reached number 1 in the charts in Ireland and 6 in the UK. Today Thin Lizzy's rocked-up version of the song is a staple of many rock bands and buskers and has been famously covered by legendary American heavy metal band Metallica.

"Sometimes I go out [on stage] and go completely berserk ... I get as heavily into what I'm doing as when I used to be a kid playing cowboys. Anybody can be anybody in rock and roll. It allows for all these people to exist within it and live out their fantasies."
— Phil Lynott

However, as a cover of a folk song, "Whiskey in the Jar" didn't really fit with Thin Lizzy's other music. This made it difficult for them to build a following based on that success. They went on for several years playing as a support act for other bands, often performing to small crowds who did not care about them and were waiting for the main act. A lot of bands who get stuck at that stage of development give up, but Phil raised his game as a performer so that the crowds couldn't ignore him.

Finally in 1976 Thin Lizzy released their breakthrough 6th studio album, *Jailbreak*. Singles like "The Boys Are Back in Town" and "Jailbreak" were big hits and saw them shoot to international stardom. By now Phil was a ready-made rock star who knew how to win over audiences and was ready to rock the world. Over the next few years Thin Lizzy toured extensively in the United States and gained a level of success in America that no Irish band had

Dove

Dove were a group of young singers and rappers from Dublin. The band formed in 1997 and was named after *dubh*, which is Irish for Black. The group was formed by Graham Cruz along with Hazel Kaneswaran, Don Ade and Lorna Davis. All members of the band were from multi-racial backgrounds, which was a new thing in Ireland, and they made a lot of headlines.

After several successful singles the band became well known in the Irish music scene. Then their cover of the Crowded House classic "Don't Dream It's Over" reached 6th place in the Irish charts.

Despite their early success in Ireland the band split in 2000. Hazel Kaneswaran would go on to pursue a solo music and TV career.

had before. Back in Europe they headlined the massive Reading Festival in England.

Phil used a lot of Celtic mythology in his songs, which stood out in the hard-rock genre that was dominated by British and American bands. Thin Lizzy's playing style was defined by having two lead guitars, a great rock drummer and Phil's charismatic stagecraft and distinctive deep voice. These elements created a sound that was made for live performances in big venues like stadiums and open-air festivals.

In 1978 the band released *Live and Dangerous*, which is often claimed to be the greatest live album of all time.

> "I am egotistical, that I won't deny ... I do think I'm good – in fact, I know I'm good ... but I know that I don't appeal to everybody." — Phil Lynott

Phil released two solo albums, and his solo single "Old Town", with its video showing Phil walking around 1980s Dublin, has become an iconic Irish pop song. He also published two books of his poetry.

Phil had a tumultuous personal life. He struggled with drug and alcohol addiction, which led to the breakdown of his marriage and the deterioration of his health. He collapsed on Christmas day in 1985 and was found by his mother who, with his ex-wife, brought him to the hospital. Phil Lynott died of sepsis and pneumonia on 4 January 1986, at the age of 36.

Phil Lynott blazed a trail for other Irish musicians who achieved international success after him. In 2005 a statue to Phil was unveiled on Harry Street, just off Grafton Street in Dublin. The bass guitar in the statue's hands always has a number of plectrums stuck in its strings, put there by fans who came to pay their respects to a Black Irish legend.

Blessing Dada

Mental health and disability activist

"Go where you are celebrated"

Trigger warning: This chapter covers topics that include mental illness and suicide

AS A MENTAL HEALTH advocate who is open about her own Autism and chronic illnesses, Blessing Dada has overcome near impossible odds. She has survived poverty, homelessness, bullying and abuse. Not only has she survived, she's also brought other people along on her journey.

Born and raised in Dublin to Nigerian parents, Blessing was the eldest of four children. Autistic and chronically ill, Blessing struggled in childhood. She had a difficult home life and experienced bullying outside the home. At school Blessing experienced racism from White people, but also discrimination from within the Black community. Without good role models in her life and unable to put her feelings into words until she was older, Blessing immersed herself in the world of books and discovered her love of writing at a young age.

Blessing believes that a culture of toxic masculinity was at the root of some of the problems she experienced and made it hard for her Autism diagnosis to be accepted.

Sport was Blessing's other escape from her problems. Growing up, she played basketball, football, Gaelic football, camogie, athletics and badminton. But her athletic journey came to an end when she was diagnosed with the first of her five chronic illnesses, fibromyalgia, when she was just 15 years old. Soon after this, she was also diagnosed with myalgic encephalomyelitis (ME), along with three other chronic illnesses. Blessing says that "sport was her life". Both her mental health and her grades became worse after her illnesses forced her to stop playing sport.

Blessing's physical health got a lot worse during secondary school and she often had to go into hospital. She missed a lot of days of school. Depside achieving all As on her Junior Cert, she failed her Leaving Cert and doesn't remember her graduation because she fainted during the ceremony.

Some CHRONIC ILLNESSES, like fibromyalgia and ME, cause people to be fatigued and experience low energy levels a lot of the time.

As a teenager, Blessing found it hard to access help and treatment for her mental health problems. She feels that she was "let down by the system" until she turned 18.

Activism found Blessing when she embarked on a campaign for climate action at school. While she was campaigning to raise awareness about climate change, Blessing lost three friends to suicide between the ages of 13 and 15. That terrible experience made her shift her focus from climate to mental health activism.

Blessing believes that because she is Black, her Autistic traits weren't interpreted properly. She was often seen as an "angry Black woman" during a meltdown, rather than an Autistic person who was struggling.

Blessing knew that "something was wrong" during her teens, but she didn't have the right words to talk about it. When she first came across the words "mental health", "something just clicked". But when she searched on the internet for mental health advice, the information she found was not relevant to Black people. Speakers came to her school to talk about mental health, but none of them were disabled or people of colour. When Blessing tried to talk about the effect of racism on her mental health, people acted like her feelings weren't valid. She knew it was important for others like her to see themselves represented, so she began to talk about her experiences on social media. That's how she became a mental health activist.

Blessing shares her story so that other young people who are going through similar struggles do not feel alone. She wants to help people of every race and identity to think and talk about mental health and disability. She thinks things are starting to change in schools around discussions about mental health, anti-racism, neurodiversity and disability, but there is much more work to be done. Blessing writes for mental health and youth organisations and creates educational resources via her social media platforms. She lobbies for change by speaking with politicians. She also works with a number of mental health charities to raise awareness for Black mental health.

Blessing has always loved her Blackness and her Nigerian heritage and she has always loved being Irish. She feels very Black and very Irish, although those two identities have not always come together in harmony. But Blessing is beginning to feel "at peace" with her identity now in her 20s. She says, "I'm just me," and no longer tries to define herself by society's standards.

When the Black Lives Matter movement kicked off in Ireland, Blessing found herself wondering, *Which Black lives are we talking about?* Not all Black people have the same experiences. Blessing focuses on the experiences of people who represent multiple identities, like people of colour who are also disabled, as well as those who are in the LGBTQIA+ community. Blessing has set up a fund for people who are struggling and offers assistance when they reach out to her. She believes that if you have a bit of extra money at the end of the week, there are plenty of people out there who need it.

Blessing's hope for Ireland is for people to "go where they're celebrated, not where they're tolerated". She wants to see more people embrace the "full extent of their existence without having to feel out of place". She thinks a lot of people in Ireland are feeling disconnected, and that if we could all work on being "really there for each other", we would all be more in touch with our humanity.

James Lumumba

James Lumumba lives in Tallaght, Dublin. He is a mental health advocate and the host of the *Don't Be Afraid To Talk* podcast, which focuses on mental health.

The topics James discusses with guests on his podcast range from biological influences on mental health to the everyday experiences of people who may have suffered with mental health issues. These conversations break down barriers and help people to better understand mental health.

James takes joy from working with humanitarian organisations in Africa and Dublin. He puts a special emphasis on Black mental health and wants to see more conversation happening around this topic.

Lawson Mpame

Style icon

"Make enough noise so that they can't ignore you"

EVERYONE THOUGHT Lawson Mpame would follow in his father's footsteps and become a lawyer. Never one to simply do what was expected of him, Lawson decided that he would study biopharmaceuticals and pursue a career in medicine. Fashion had been in his life from a young age, with two very fashionable parents (his mother made clothes for her own stores back in Zimbabwe). But it wasn't until he started posting about his own fashion sense on social media that Lawson realised being a stylist and creative director was the career for him.

*Lawson's menswear style tips can be found on Instagram at @lawsofstyle_*

In the early days of Lawson's foray into fashion in 2015, his inspiration was his father's sense of style: fully tailored suits for a clean, crisp, dapper businessman look. Starting small, Lawson just posted about his daily outfits and offered style tips. He was quickly noticed by Louis Copeland, the famous high-end men's clothing store in Dublin. They asked him to work with them on their "made-to-measure" service and help them tap into a younger customer base. His first collaboration secured, with a free suit his only payment, Lawson was on his way to becoming a fashion icon.

Making connections in the industry led Lawson to his next collaboration: with international clothing brand Tommy Hilfiger. That was the jumping-off point for everything that was to follow.

In the Irish fashion world, Lawson was a young Black Irish person in a sea of White faces and this made people notice him. He was asked to participate in numerous collaborations, but his first paying gig was with the famous Irish retailer Penneys. Despite his early success with big-name brands, it wasn't until he actually got paid for his work that Lawson realised that working in fashion was something he could do as a career. Since then, Lawson has worked with a number of global clothing brands and retailers and even appeared in online and TV ads.

For a long time, Lawson was the only Black person at many fashion events. While he was aware of the significance of being

Oyindamola (Zeda) Animashaun

Oyindamola, also known as Oyin and Zeda the Architect, is a stylist, film director, creative director and costume designer. She is the fashion editor of VIP Publishing, and has contributed to some huge projects with *Stellar* and *VIP* magazines. Zeda is also a stylist to some famous Irish celebrities like Erica Cody and Aimée.

Having moved to Ireland at a young age from Nigeria, Zeda found inspiration close to home in her parents, whom she credits with cultivating her love of fashion. Beginning her journey into the industry during college, Zeda has made her way from college fashion shows to personal shopping on the high street to prestigious magazine shoots. She's a photographer and cinematographer as well, who is always looking to highlight the diversity in Ireland in every project.

When asked for advice for other young creatives, Zeda has said: "If you have an idea, just do it. You don't even need to show it to the world, nobody even needs to see it, but just do it because you will learn something new from doing whatever that 'it' is." She hopes many more Black Irish creatives will heed this advice and join her in Ireland's growing fashion scene.

invited to events that were previously not open to Black people, he couldn't help feeling alienated and lonely at times. He struggled without a mentor – someone that he could look up to and seek guidance from. He also started to notice that colleagues would often separate him from other Black people that were trying to get into the industry. He was often told that he was not the same as "those other Black people". There were comments about Black people being "too ghetto" and "too loud", but Lawson was often told that *he* was different. Comments like these might have been intended as compliments to Lawson, but they felt like microaggressions.

After the Black Lives Matter movement took the world by storm in 2020, Lawson saw a change in the amount of representation in the fashion industry. A lot of brands started to diversify and include models and styles from a variety of Black identities. Lawson enjoyed a lot of success during this time. He's thrilled to see more faces like his in the industry since that shift. As a creative director, Lawson has had the chance to step behind the camera and organise a team of people working on fashion shoots and campaigns, and he's excited to see diverse crews doing this work now.

Growing up amongst communities of Black people in Galway and Dublin, Lawson didn't experience a lot of overt or direct racism, but he can recall a few isolated incidents that had an effect on him. From being locked out of a taxi to being racially profiled by police, Lawson knows that his Blackness has definitely influenced how he has been treated in certain situations. In one way, Lawson has used his sense of style to help him avoid being targeted by the police because he knows that he is more likely to be stopped if he is wearing a hoodie or tracksuit bottoms. When he wears his suits and high-end clothing items he is rarely stopped. While this is something Lawson can afford to do because of the privilege he has gained from working in the fashion industry, he says that this doesn't take away from the fact that the racial profiling of Black people is a real problem.

While he considers himself Irish, Lawson is open about his struggles with his Black and Irish identity. He is often asked where he is from, which makes him feel that his Irishness is not accepted. Things are not getting easier with the current rise in anti-immigration protests in Ireland and Lawson finds it difficult to be proud of his Irish identity at the moment. "Why should I fly a flag for a country that doesn't even want me here?" he asks himself regularly.

RACIAL PROFILING is when a person is stopped or hassled by police, security guards or other authority figures on account of their race. People of colour experience profiling from law enforcement in many countries.

Lawson knows that he is not alone in how he feels. He hopes that things get better soon in Ireland, and he knows that that lies in the hands of the young people of Ireland taking a stand against racism. What makes Ireland beautiful is the fact it has traditionally been a welcoming place, and Lawson hopes it can reclaim that aspect of its identity soon so that everyone can finally be accepted. He looks forward to being able to fully reclaim his Black and Irish identity in the near future. At the moment, Lawson is looking abroad for opportunities because of a decrease in work in Ireland and the increase in anti-immigrant sentiments.

Even after finding success, Lawson still struggles to wrap his head around the fact that he is now a professional creative.

He loves his work and feels lucky to be paid for something that "doesn't feel like a job half the time". The beauty of his field is that he is able to explore so many different opportunities not just in fashion, but also in TV and other media.

Lawson's motto has always been "make enough noise so that they can't ignore you" and he plans to continue making noise. He wants young Black Irish aspiring fashion creatives to do the same. He's currently working on a project to help young people who want to get into the industry get connected to mentors and contacts so that they can get a sense of the work and start networking. His advice for young people is to never be afraid to ask for help from others in the line of work you want to be part of, and don't stop until you are in the spaces you belong in. Once you're there, make sure to return the favour and help other young creatives to come in behind you.

Yemi Adenuga

Ireland's first Black female councillor

"You hold the key to your life"

THE ADENUGA name might sound familiar if you've ever watched the Irish version of the show *Gogglebox*. Yemi and her family represented their hometown of Navan, County Meath, by watching shows together on TV. Yemi is proud that they are known locally as "the Navan Adenugas" – Adenuga is a Navan name now, whether Navan likes it or not!

LOCAL COUNCILS in Ireland make decisions about local things like social housing, libraries, and environmental protection. They are made up of democratically elected councillors.

When Yemi first arrived in Ireland in 2000 from her native Nigeria, the country really lived up to its reputation as the land of *céad míle fáilte*: "a hundred thousand welcomes". Yemi saw Ireland as a land of opportunity, filled with warm and helpful people. She remembers hearing an ad on the radio aimed at newly arrived immigrants offering a service that would connect them with Irish families. If it wasn't for that service she probably wouldn't be where she is today: Ireland's first Black female councillor.

From a young age Yemi knew that she "owned the key" to her own life, and that unless she gave someone else that key, they couldn't get in. Nobody else could tell her how to live her life. She needed to make sure that she was always "holding that key", and to only give it to people she knew she could trust.

In Nigeria, Yemi had her own media company, and she ran Nigeria's most successful talk radio show, *Sharing with Yemi*. Yemi wasn't afraid to tackle all kinds of difficult issues on her show, and sometimes she "stepped on toes" and called people out. As a result she was the target of police brutality and home invasions, so that Nigeria became an unsafe place for her family. She and her husband needed to find somewhere safe to raise their children. Yemi felt that her heart was called to Ireland and she followed that call. She knows now that she will grow old here and has even picked out the plot where she will be buried in Ireland. That's commitment!

Now Councillor Yemi Adenuga represents the Navan Municipal District as part of the Meath County Council. As well

Uruemu Adejnmi

Ireland's first black female mayor, Uruemu was elected Mayor of Longford County Council in 2021 after starting her journey in politics in 2016. Uruemu is dedicated to working with diverse community and migrant groups and helping them access services and support in Ireland.

Originally from Nigeria, Uruemu knows first-hand what the African Irish community needs and how best to support them within the Irish system. She knows that there is a level of mistrust amongst her community and the people who serve them, like the police force, because of their experiences back home. But she also knows that it's vital that migrants engage with local services in order to feel safe and supported where they live.

Uruemu would love to see more political involvement from people from migrant backgrounds. She knows that by getting involved people can make a real difference in their local communities and even on the national level, but the first step is learning more about the political system and getting out and voting.

as a politician, she is also a community activist and creator of programmes for migrants and the youth of Ireland. She has founded organisations including Boys to Men, which helps young boys become good men and encourages men to be mentors for young boys; and Girls' Club, which inspires girls to find confidence and develop their identities in a healthy way.

Yemi's childhood was not easy. She was the 16th of 27 children in her family, and her mother was the 7th wife of her father. Because of customs in Nigeria at the time, and because she was a daughter of her father's last wife, Yemi was told that she and her sisters from the same mother wouldn't achieve anything in life. When Yemi was 13 she found her mother crying because her father's family told her that she would never amount to anything. She wanted to make her mother stop crying, so she made a promise. She promised her mother that she and her sisters would be so successful that people would regret saying anything bad about them. That promise became the foundation of everything Yemi has done in her life, especially her dedication to helping other women and young girls realise their potential.

FINE GAEL is one of Ireland's largest political parties and has been in government in Ireland many times since Irish independence. In 2020 Fine Gael formed an alliance with its historic rival party, Fianna Fáil, as well as the Green Party, to form a new government.

Yemi never really planned on a career in politics, but when the Fine Gael political party approached her about joining in 2018, she saw it as a way to do more of the community work that she was already involved with. Yemi wants to be a positive influence on society and ensure that young people are heard and that their issues are addressed. She saw politics as the platform that she could use to pursue those goals.

While Ireland lived up to its reputation of being a welcoming place, life here hasn't been without challenges. When the family first arrived, Yemi's daughter was the only Black student in her school. She experienced racial bullying, with other kids calling her "black monkey" and saying that she "lived in a tree". Yemi has also experienced racism countless times as a public figure. She was blackmailed and had the lives of her children threatened. Instead of letting those who threatened her win, she reported the incidents to An Garda Síochána and went about her business.

Yemi wants to help Irish people as well as migrants to have conversations that might sometimes be tricky. For example, she wants to explain to migrants the reasoning behind the classic question "Where are you from?" but also help White Irish people understand why that question can be a sore point for those who don't appear "typically Irish", because it suggests that they are not accepted as Irish.

Yemi is worried that Ireland has forgotten how to be curious and keep growing and learning from people who come here. As a self-described "let's solve the problem kind of person", Yemi is working on a project at the moment called Culture Pals that will connect recently arrived immigrants to others who have been living in Ireland for some time.

Have you ever heard the term "unconscious bias"? It means that we have opinions or ideas about people based on incomplete information, and that we judge other people based on these ideas and opinions. We all have biases. It's just how our brains are wired. But Yemi says that it's time to stop calling bias "unconscious" and to "Wake up and be conscious!" The moment you become aware of your bias, you can no longer call it *unconscious*. Yemi believes that when you meet a new person, you should not let your mind run wild about who you think they might be, and instead open your mind to listening, learning and hearing what they have to say. When we do that, we gain so much

Yemi would love to see more women in politics in Ireland. She encourages young girls to find seats in places of power.

by getting to know a new person who might think and do things differently than us. Connecting with others like this helps us build cultures and communities.

Rotimi Adebari

Rotimi was elected Mayor of Portlaoise, County Laois, in 2007 and is the first African man to be an elected mayor in Ireland. Before arriving in Ireland, Rotimi earned a degree in economics from Benin University. He fled Nigeria because of religious persecution in 2000. He and his family settled in Portlaoise in 2003 and he went on to study at Dublin City University, earning a master's degree in intercultural studies in 2004, all while volunteering in local community organisations and starting an integration initiative called Voice Across Cultures.

Rotimi has also been a radio host and a non-profit organiser and was chosen as a jury member for the European Programme for Integration and Migration. He has earned numerous awards and was appointed as a Peace Commissioner in 2012.

Yemi feels African but also Irish. She has been part of Irish society for over 20 years. Navan is her base, her home, where she feels an immense sense of belonging. Yemi wants to show people from marginalised communities that this sense of belonging is possible to achieve in Ireland. She also wants immigrants to understand that you can't always just wait for things to come to you: sometimes you have to take them for yourself. She says that no one in Navan was offering her "Navan citizenship": she had to take it and claim it and make it her own.

Being Black and Irish is the best of both worlds, according to Yemi. This dual identity lets her bring her learnings from being an Irish woman together with her experiences of being an African woman to create something really fantastic. She is excited to see what the Black and Irish community comes up with next. It's a new identity, it's fresh, and it's still being defined, which is exciting and invigorating. It means that there is an amazing opportunity to create something totally new and decide what it should be from the ground up. For Yemi, it's up to young Black Irish people to take this opportunity to build up their identity and community themselves and make it their own. This will help all Black Irish people to feel the sense of belonging that everyone needs to feel safe, secure and happy.

Yemi's hope for Ireland is that it becomes a place where everyone is respected and treated with dignity, a country that becomes truly inclusive by letting people from diverse backgrounds sit at the table where decisions are made. She hopes Ireland will be a place where her grandsons are able to walk the streets and feel safe. She believes that all of this will happen. Yemi herself would like to be remembered as the person who always found the solutions to challenges, who inspired women and young people in Ireland and across the globe, and as a woman who was able to make her family proud through every action she took to impact her community in Navan. For Yemi it always comes back to Navan!

Patrick Martins

Actor

"Putting diversity on the national stage"

WHEN PATRICK MARTINS was 12, his mother brought him and his siblings to try out for a Disney show. While nothing came of the audition, the experience sparked something in Patrick. His mother recognised that acting was a potential talent that she should encourage in her son. In 2022, Patrick took the lead role in a play called *An Octoroon* at Ireland's national theatre, the Abbey Theatre in Dublin.

THE OCTOROON was a play written in the 1850s by Irish playwright Dion Boucicault about slave owners in the USA. *An Octoroon* is an adaptation of Boucicault's play made by a contemporary Black American writer, Branden Jacobs-Jenkins, that explores questions of race and the representation of diversity in theatre. An "octoroon" was a term for somebody with one-eighth Black ancestry.

Patrick was born in Nigeria and moved to Ireland when he was 5 years old. He grew up in Ireland and recently moved to London to pursue acting opportunities. Patrick had an enjoyable experience growing up in Ireland and looks back fondly on his childhood. He made amazing friends who helped him to settle in when he moved to the country.

Most professional actors enter drama school at a young age and spend a lot of their early years singing, dancing or performing on stage. But while Patrick's earliest memory of acting is his mother rounding up him and his siblings and bringing them to that audition for a Disney show, which she had heard about on the radio, he didn't begin to formally study the art form until the age of 17.

Most of the Nigerian parents Patrick knew wanted to see their child follow a traditional route and become a lawyer or a doctor. But his mother always understood him as a person and was able to spot his talents. Patrick remembers the day that his mother suggested acting to him. He had come home from a stressful day during his Leaving Cert. He didn't know what he wanted to do or where he wanted to go. His mother told him that he was always entertaining people and making them laugh. She suggested he should go for it.

Patrick auditioned for the Lir Academy in Dublin, which had a yearly intake of 16 students, 8 boys and 8 girls. He was absolutely delighted when he was accepted. It was a 3-year course. After graduating in 2019 he was cast as the lead in the National Theatre of Scotland play *Enough of Him*. He also started getting TV work in Ireland and the UK.

Shauna Harris

Shauna Harris is a Dublin-based actress who has worked extensively in theatre, as well as in film and television. In addition to acting, Shauna also sings and dances and is a multidisciplinary performer. Her most well-known project to date is *Hive City Legacy: Dublin Chapter*, which won awards at the Dublin Fringe Festival in 2022.

Shauna is Mixed-Race and often speaks about her experiences with representation in her industry. In addition to performing, Shauna also has a degree in politics, international relations and social justice from University College Dublin. Whenever her interest in social justice coincides with her passion for performing, Shauna jumps at the opportunity to contribute to those projects.

For Patrick, his proudest moment came on the Abbey Theatre stage with *An Octoroon*. The cast in the play was very diverse and it was one of the first times Ireland's national theatre had put on a show like that. This was so important for Patrick, as he knows that Ireland is becoming more diverse. From the stage, he could see that the audience was diverse, too, and he hopes that seeing that play encouraged people to get into the industry.

The **ABBEY THEATRE** is Ireland's national theatre. It was co-founded by the great Irish poet WB Yeats and has played a role in the national conversation about Irish identity and for over 100 years.

Patrick's advice to young people in Ireland is to keep pushing and to be resilient. He understands that people from different minority groups will face difficulties, and that at times it will be tough not to be discouraged. Patrick believes that if you really want something it will be yours. Whether you have to wait one day or 10 years, it will eventually come if you continue to work on it every day and be patient.

Controversy struck the Irish Times Theatre Awards when only the two White cast members from the 10-person diverse cast of *An Octoroon* were nominated for awards. It was seen as a "missing the point" issue on behalf of the awards judges. Patrick as well as others involved with the play like Esosa Igharo gave brave statements that resonated well with the theatre community.

Patrick has many hopes for his industry and for Ireland. He hopes to see diverse work continuously being created. He wants to see talents from diverse communities being showcased. For Patrick it is vitally important not only that diversity appears in front of the camera but that more people join the acting industry as a whole. He wants to see more writers, producers and crew coming from different backgrounds. Right now, Patrick believes that when people discuss diverse talent, their eyes are fixed on the UK. He wants to see Ireland included in that conversation.

Rhasidat Adeleke

Record-breaking sprinter

"Always in first"

NOT LONG AGO, Rhasidat Adeleke was racing and beating all the boys in her class at school. She would turn up to PE or Sports Day and her classmates could count on her to win everything. Fast forward 6 years and she is smashing athletics records on a regular basis. She is Ireland's fastest woman, holding national records in 60m, 200m and 400m distances. She has won gold at the European Championships. And she's only 21 years of age.

Rhasidat was born and raised in Dublin to Nigerian parents. Growing up in Tallaght, Rhasidat took part in many different sports, including camogie, Gaelic football, soccer, badminton and volleyball, before finding her true passion: athletics. When she was 12 years old, her PE teacher encouraged her to join a running club. She got better and better each year. Her winning streak started when she was still competing at the junior level.

Rhasidat has been winning medals in both Irish and European competitions since she was in her teens. In 2017, aged 14, she won a sprint double at the Irish schools championship. She then competed at the European Youth Olympic Festival and won silver in the 200 metres. In 2018, she won gold in the 200m race at the European Under-18 Championships. In 2019, she went back to the European Youth Olympic Festival and won the 100m and 200m sprint double. Back home in Ireland, at the age of 18, Rhasidat won her first senior national outdoor title. She then went on to win the 100m and 200m sprint double at the European U20 Championships with blistering paces in both races. She was the first woman to win this double since 2011.

In 2021, Rhasidat was offered the opportunity to move to the United States and compete at the college level while attending the University of Texas in Austin. Moving to the US, the historic home of some of the fastest female athletes in history, was an exciting but daunting move for her. She had been used to winning at the Irish and European levels and needed to "get used to losing". At first, losing races that she had won comfortably in Europe was difficult for Rhasidat. It wasn't easy to come in dead last when she was used to blowing away the competition. She was hard on herself, but she quickly learned that it was important to have "short term memory" and not to dwell on the losses because another race was always just around the corner. She began to see each competition as an opportunity to improve and learn and do better next time, and she certainly has learned to do better. A

Israel Olatunde

Ireland's fastest man, Israel Olatunde was born in Drogheda to Nigerian parents and raised in Dundalk.

Growing up Israel played soccer and Gaelic football. He was always the fastest player on his team and had obvious athletic ability from a very young age. He looked up to his older sister Sharon, who was a huge influence on his decision to take up athletics and become serious about running.

At secondary school Israel encountered coach Gerry McArdle. McArdle had a profound impact on Israel's career and to this day they have a close friendship.

At his first indoor competition, Israel won the junior (under-20) national title in the 60m race, with a time of 6.99 seconds. He has since been crowned Ireland's fastest man with a new a new Irish 100m record of 10.17 seconds, set in 2022.

lot better. In 2022, in her first senior European Championships, Rhasidat placed 5th in the 400m final, setting an Irish record of 50.53 seconds.

In January of 2023, Rhasidat beat her own national indoor 200m record with a time of 22.52 seconds: the fastest time a European woman has run since 2003. Rhasidat also set a new Irish indoor record in the 400m at 50.45 seconds. Then she beat her own record, resetting the mark at 50.33 seconds. The following month, she ran 50.45 seconds at the National Collegiate Athletic Association (NCAA) indoors final, earning the silver medal to become the first Irish athlete to win a medal in an NCAA sprint event. In addition to these solo successes, Rhasidat has also won a number of medals and set records as part of her college relay team.

Rhasidat is now making a big career move: she is going to turn professional in the lead up to the next summer Olympics in 2024 in Paris. This means she needs to put her studies on hold while she pursues her Olympic dreams, but she knows that this next step is important for her running career and she's looking forward to representing Ireland on the Olympic stage.

Being able to represent Ireland abroad and on an international stage is important to Rhasidat because she is proud of her Irish identity. Her advice for young athletes is to try everything and to not become too concerned with success. She says that it's important to not only be successful at what you choose to do, but to choose to do something because you love doing it.

Rhasidat thinks that young athletes should also remember to stay involved in the social aspect of sport. She loves being part of a team and meeting people from all over the world. She believes there is so much more to sport than athleticism and winning. Rhasidat loves that sport brings people together. She also believes that mental health is an important part of any competitive sport. You must be ready to lose and not let it get you down. Instead, you need to let the losses motivate you to do even better next time. Rhasidat hopes that all young athletes remember to only stay in a sport as long as they benefit from it and make sure they get the most from it while they can.

Unfortunately, despite her massive success, Rhasidat has had some negative racist comments on social media that question her Irishness. Rhasidat tries to focus on the much more frequent positive feedback she receives. She hopes that Ireland can become a more united and accepting place, and that the celebrations of the positive achievements of Irish people will far outweigh any negative voices in future.

Rhasidat knows that her 15-year-old self would be proud of her achievements so far. She hopes that she can be an inspiration for aspiring young Black Irish athletes to pursue their dreams.

Jude Hughes

Diversity activist

"Always on the side of the oppressed"

JUDE HUGHES has always been a fighter. He is an activist who stands up for what he believes is right. He built organisations to tackle inequality in Irish society. From forming the group Harmony in the 1980s to getting involved with the Association of Mixed Race Irish, Jude is never too far from the battle for human rights and dignity.

Jude Hughes was born in 1941 in Dublin. He was raised in three different institutions. He has some fond memories of his childhood. Children would play with him and be fascinated with his hair. Families would encourage their children to befriend him and give him presents. In hindsight he recognises some problematic behaviours but he was too young to understand them.

Jude moved to a Christian Brothers institution around the age of 8. Some of the brothers didn't like seeing Jude getting positive attention and would go out of their way to try to make his life difficult. Groups of boys would often be taken to Croke Park. One day Jude was supposed to go on a trip, but a brother decided not to allow him to go, for no reason. Jude was made to stay behind while others got to go and enjoy the day. When a senior teacher found Jude had been left behind, he was furious with the other brother and that never happened again. This taught Jude that there are good people in the world.

The Christian Brothers religious community ran a large number of schools and institutions in Ireland. A lot of stories of abuse and violence suffered at those places have come out in recent decades.

In his teenage years, Jude began to experience some racialised issues. He faced name-calling, threats and being excluded. But he remained strong. He coped with the abuse by focusing on himself and getting involved with sports. He began playing basketball and tennis. Even today, in his 80s, Jude is an avid tennis player.

As an adult Jude trained as a tailor. He started his own business in the 1970s. He has been working for himself for nearly 50 years and runs a shop on Abbey Street in Dublin. Jude remembers facing discrimination when he started out in business. People would come running down the stairs into his business but "freeze up" as soon as they saw him. They would say that they thought they were in the wrong place, but Jude would assure them that they weren't. Once they gave him a chance, Jude would do a fine job with their clothes and they would often refer friends and family to him. One of Jude's biggest issues now is that he has too much work!

Annie Yellowe Palma

Annie Yellowe Palma was born in 1962 in Liverpool to an Irish mother and Nigerian father. She grew up in Portadown, County Armagh, Northern Ireland, with her mother and siblings. Annie's family were staunchly Protestant, and she was raised in Northern Ireland during the height of the Troubles.

Annie was a poet and an author. She published two books including *For the Love of a Mother: The Black Children of Ulster*. This book explored her and her family's experiences as a Black family in the 1960s and 70s, navigating sectarian violence as well as racial issues. Annie passed away in 2022.

The **CIVIL RIGHTS** movement in America took place in the 1950s and 60s, calling for an end to laws that discriminated against Black people. Among its leaders was Dr Martin Luther King Jr. In Ireland and around the world, people marched in solidarity with what was happening in the USA. In Northern Ireland members of the Catholic community were inspired to begin a Civil Rights movement to oppose discrimination against themselves.

When Jude witnessed the growing Civil Rights movement in the US in the 1960s he felt a strong urge to fight for what is right, and he joined the solidarity marches that took place in Ireland. It was an easy choice for him as to what side he was going to be on: he is always on the side of the oppressed. He couldn't believe that there were laws in parts of the world that stopped people from living normal lives or partaking equally in society.

Jude was also inspired by the amount of African countries that were standing up for themselves and breaking free of colonial ties. Their fight encouraged Jude to lead a charge in Ireland for justice and equality. This was the beginning of Jude's career as an activist.

In 1987 Jude put out a call to all people who had experienced racism in Ireland to come to Dublin's Wynn's Hotel on 15 September. At that time there was a rise in hateful rhetoric beginning to creep in in Ireland, so Jude hoped some people would come along and share their experiences. He was shocked when he arrived at the hotel and the room was so packed he couldn't even get in the door!

Seeing how much demand there was for a group to address racial issues in Ireland, Jude founded an organisation called Harmony. Harmony worked to bring different people and different cultures together. They teamed up with multiple embassies and ran many events. Their work led to the Irish government appointing the first Minister for Equality in 1994, the Labour Party's Mervyn Taylor. This was a huge achievement for Jude's group. Harmony ended in 2000 but it would not be the last organisation that Jude would play a major part in, and he was influential in the establishment of the Association of Mixed Race Irish.

Jude felt disconnected from his African heritage from a young age but he visited Africa multiple times. He reckons that anyone of African descent who is in a similar situation to him should travel to Africa at least once in their lifetime. Jude is a collector of African wares and has a cool collection of tapestries, statues and masks.

Jude is a wise man and has a lot he wishes to give back to younger generations. He believes that getting involved in your community is one of the best things you can do in your life as it can give you a real sense of purpose. He understands that a lot of young Black people in Ireland can sometimes struggle to fit in. He was once in that position himself, and he knows how important it is to have a sense of belonging. His advice is to always be yourself and involve yourself in your community.

THE ASSOCIATION OF MIXED RACE IRISH campaigned on the abuses faced by Mixed-Race people in the institutions in Ireland such as the Mother-and-Baby Homes. The organisation has made strides in having Mixed-Race identity recognised in Ireland and their work led to a number of reforms in how the survivors of Mother-and-Baby Homes were recognised and compensated.

Jude wants to see young Black Irish people showing their abilities, and he loves to see the likes of athlete Rhasidat Adeleke becoming such a star. He is thrilled with the level of representation the Black Irish community has in sport and is eagerly awaiting the Olympics in Paris. Jude hopes to see that level of Black representation reflected throughout our society.

Emer O'Neill

Teacher, TV presenter and activist

"Fight to get Ireland to where it should be"

TEACHER, BASKETBALL star, television presenter, children's book author, activist, mother. You could say that Emer O'Neill is quite the busy woman! It wasn't always this way. She only really started using her voice to speak out against racism in Ireland in 2020, after the murder of George Floyd and the surge in the global Black Lives Matter movement.

Growing up in Bray, County Wicklow, in the 1980s and 90s, young Emer didn't see a lot of people who looked like her. Her mother is White Irish and met her father while working in Nigeria as a volunteer nurse. Emer has felt the effects of racism from an early age, from name-calling to physical attacks. She can remember bullies who targeted her and threatened her, all because she was Black. A self-described "messer" as a kid, Emer would often be solely blamed for things that she and her friends got up to. She stood out because of the colour of her skin. She and her mother were forced to move several times before finding a safe place where Emer would be free from abuse.

> Emer thinks the reluctance to accept that people can be Irish but not White is one of the biggest problems in Ireland today.

Emer's struggles to understand her identity have caused her some mental health difficulties which she is still working on today. She is constantly asked where she is from, and despite saying that she is from Bray, strangers will often ask where she's *really* from, not believing that she's just as Irish as the next person. Her Irishness is often questioned.

Even though she experienced racism on a regular basis growing up, Emer found that it was really difficult to share those experiences with others because of a lack of understanding. She was often "gaslit" or told she was imagining things. Emer thinks that because no one around her knew what it was like to be Black or Mixed-Race that it made it more difficult for people to relate to what she was going through. It was difficult for her to put into words the feelings she had when she encountered more subtle forms of racism, like adults speaking to her in a different way to how they spoke to her friends. There was also the fear of calling even more attention to herself by talking about something that had happened to her.

Nike Adesiyan

Special education teacher Nike Adesiyan is fluent in sign language and works with students who are deaf and hard of hearing. Originally from Nigeria, Nike moved to Ireland in 1999 and was one of the first Black teachers in Ireland. She lives and works in Ennis, County Clare, and is a mother of four.

Nike describes her experiences as an educator in Ireland as a "rollercoaster". Her proudest moments as a teacher include introducing the alternative Leaving Cert Applied programme for her deaf students, and watching her students move on to third level education in a variety of fields.

Nike works hard to make sure that every learner's voice is heard and that their individual talents, gifts and creative abilities are recognised and valued because she believes that everyone deserves to have their uniqueness nurtured and celebrated. She is looking forward to the day when intercultural education is included in the curriculum of all Irish schools.

Basketball was an amazing outlet for Emer. She was tall and had a gift for athleticism, and sports provided a way to escape from the negativity and racism that often followed her. She was recruited to the Irish national basketball team in her first year of secondary school, after only taking up the sport the year before. The confidence she gained from being successful in basketball is one of the things that she credits for helping her find her way in life. "No one cared about what colour I was when I was scoring baskets," she says, recalling how liberating being on the court was for her.

Emer got an opportunity to study in the United States on a basketball scholarship. She was excited to go to America because of the diversity she knew she would find there. "I was excited to live somewhere where I wouldn't stick out," she recalls. She knew that she would not only fit in there, but also have easy access to things like Afro hair-care products and be able to get her hair done easily. However, the difficulties of being Mixed-Race followed her across the ocean. In the US people viewed her as "too Black to be White" while at the same time "too White to be Black", and she struggled to find where she belonged.

Emer spent three years in a university in Mississippi, a state notorious for its racist history. Then she moved to another college in Florida, where she finished her degree and became a PE teacher. This is where she spent the next 7 years, also completing a degree in educational leadership. Working in an American high school and meeting her first Black deputy principal gave Emer the inspiration she needed to continue working towards her goal of being a school leader.

When Emer found out she was going to be a mother while living in the US, she realised that she wanted to return home to Ireland to raise her child with the support of her family. She was nervous to return, hoping her son wouldn't face the same racism that she did growing up, but the Ireland she had seen on visits home looked and felt different than it had been a decade before. Even though she was making a life for herself in Florida, Ireland had been calling her home for some time, and she took the opportunity to return.

It was only in 2020 that Emer "removed her own muzzle" and started speaking out about racism in Ireland. She realised that she wasn't doing enough as a teacher to encourage anti-racist teaching in her school and bring more inclusion into the school curriculum. While on maternity leave with her second child, Emer decided to post a video online outlining her experiences in order to bring attention to the realities of Black and Mixed-Race people in Ireland. When that video went viral she decided continue to speak about her experiences.

During the school shutdowns because of the COVID-19 pandemic, RTÉ created a television programme for children called *Home School Hub*. Emer decided to put herself forward for the role of a PE teacher for that programme and got the part. She was an instant hit and was so proud to provide the sort of visible representation of her community on TV that she never had growing up. She was then offered a recurring presenter gig on a popular afternoon chat show and also made a docuseries for RTÉ about the importance of sports for teenage girls.

Unfortunately, it hasn't all been positive for Emer since she released her first video. She has spoken on national television and radio several times since 2020 and has even done a TED Talk, but she has also been the victim of racist bullying online. She has continued to have negative experiences, including racist graffiti in her home town of Bray, in response to her speaking out. But Emer has continued to work to bring awareness of racism in Ireland, and she is more determined than ever to spread a message of love and acceptance.

Emer helped to co-found Bray for Love, an organisation which replaced the racist graffiti in Bray with beautiful messages.

Emer's focus now is on addressing racism in Ireland directly through her speaking appearances and fiercely advocating for reform in education and industries in Ireland. She wants to bring awareness to the need for quotas in every industry so that people of all backgrounds get the same opportunities to work and excel as White people in Ireland.

QUOTAS are requirements for companies to hire certain numbers of people from marginalised backgrounds. They have been found to increase gender equality, but they can also work to make sure there are more people of colour in workplaces. Right now, there are very few people of colour working as teachers in Ireland.

Emer also wants people to understand what it's like to live as a person from a minority background so that they can empathise with their experiences instead of questioning them. She talks often about how important it is for everyone to be heard and believed. She knows how difficult it can be to talk about experiences of racism and discrimination.

At the moment, Emer feels that the Black and Irish community is in a state of trying to define its identity. Ireland will only become more and more diverse over time, and Emer hopes that one day her great-great-grandchildren will ask the question "What is racism?", because it will have completely disappeared from Irish life. In order to get there, Emer believes the government and people in power in Ireland need to help to shape this understanding by opening up spaces to people from ethnic minorities and demanding education around anti-racism and interculturalism.

Emer wants Ireland to live up to its reputation as a welcoming country, but she knows there's quite a bit of work to do to really embrace that identity. Emer is ready and willing to keep fighting to get Ireland to where she knows it should be – are you?

Dr Ebun Joseph

Founder of the first Black Studies course in Ireland

"Your voice is your power!"

EBUN JOSEPH was taught by her father that her Black skin was beautiful, and that belief has stuck with her throughout her life. She is "unapologetically Black" and loves having dual Nigerian-Irish identity. Her pride in her Blackness and her desire to share that joy with her adopted country led to her founding the Institute of Antiracism and Black Studies, as well as the first ever Black Studies university course in Ireland, at University College Dublin.

Ebun has had many jobs in her life: academic, counsellor, microbiologist, carer, career development consultant, motivational speaker. In Nigeria, her parents had wanted her to be a doctor, but with a fear of blood, she was not destined to help people in that way. But Ebun was determined to make a difference in people's lives. After first working as a scientist, when she moved to Ireland from Nigeria in 2002 she retrained as a counsellor. She chose this path because she found that she was often the person that others would go to for advice and to tell their stories.

The **INSTITUTE OF ANTIRACISM AND BLACK STUDIES** in Dublin offers training to organisations and companies about racism and diversity, and runs a campaign aimed at reducing the unemployment level of Black people in Ireland.

Ireland is a small enough place that a person doesn't get lost, but also big enough to offer plenty of opportunities. Ebun felt it was the perfect place for her to start again. But it was only when she moved to Ireland that she discovered that she had the label of "Black woman". She had never thought of herself in this way before.

Having to deal with this new way of thinking about her identity had an effect on Ebun. She realised that she now found herself in a society that did not have high expectations for Black people – and that she needed to change this. She promised herself that she would never live a life that was less than what she had had back in Nigeria. If she had a car and a house in Nigeria, then she would have at least the same or better in Ireland. She never accepted the low expectations that were put on her by those around her; instead, she maintained her own high expectations for herself and rose above.

Ebun also began volunteering when she moved to Ireland. She feels that she "brought that spirit from Africa" to Ireland because she had done a lot of social work in Nigeria and was used to helping and supporting others. She volunteered with her church and with some other organisations, doing things like helping drug users who were living on the street. This volunteer work brought her to know and understand Irish society in a deeper way.

As a career development consultant, Ebun helped people find jobs that matched their skill sets and passions. She noticed that when a Black person came to her for help, it would often take a long time to find them a job. It didn't matter how much training or how many degrees those from African backgrounds had, it was incredibly difficult to find an employer that would take them on. This inequality made Ebun decide to focus her research on the experiences of Black men in Ireland, which ultimately led to her future work as an activist.

Ebun founded the first Black Studies module in Ireland in 2018 in

BLACK STUDIES is an academic discipline which explores the history, literature, culture and more of Black people in Africa and around the world. Today Black Studies courses can be found in Ireland at University College Dublin and Trinity College Dublin.

University College Dublin. As a lecturer at UCD, several students have told her that she is the first Black teacher they ever had. She wants to make sure that her students learn about the positive experiences of Black people and not just the negative things that have happened throughout history to Black people. She wants Black people to be proud and to know all of the amazing things that they have accomplished.

Ebun wants all young Black people to know that they should never give up their voice. She says "Your voice is your power!" She is delighted to see how successful some of her former students have been and looks forward to many more to come. She is excited for the younger generation of Black Irish people who have had the privilege of being born and growing up in Ireland and have a new way of navigating the world around them. She'd love for this community to define for themselves what it means to be truly Black and Irish — which is something that only they can do. Because Ireland is home for so many young Black Irish people (many of whom have parents who were raised elsewhere), they need to really define and understand their identity in a way that works for them.

Ireland has been ahead of the curve on many social issues, like marriage equality and supporting Ukraine through their current crisis, and Ebun hopes that this country can continue to set the trend on issues of racism. To do this, anti-racism and Black Studies need to be taught to young people so that they grow up to be anti-racist and show the world how to be truly inclusive and make everyone feel like they belong.

Dami Hope

Love Island **contestant and celebrity influencer**

"Never be afraid to make friends"

WHEN YOU THINK of Irish reality TV personalities, you can't help but mention Dami Hope. Dami captured Irish imaginations in the summer of 2022 on the hit series *Love Island*. Although he already had some profile for his fashion flair, he really showed off his big personality on the show. After finishing third alongside his partner, Indiyah Polack, Dami has remained in the spotlight and is now a big name on the Irish celebrity scene.

Dami moved to Ireland at the age of three. His family are Yoruba, a large tribe from Nigeria, and Dami still visits Nigeria regularly. His family worked hard to keep him in touch with his Nigerian heritage. They would speak Yoruba, cook traditional Nigerian food often and ensure he was well connected with his church life.

The **YORUBA** are the second-largest ethnic group in Nigeria. There are over 48 million Yoruba in Nigeria – that's almost 10 times the whole population of Ireland! Yoruba people also live in neighbouring African countries, and the area inhabited by them all together is sometimes known as "Yorubaland".

Dami grew up in New Ross, County Wexford, and he mostly has positive memories of the area, which he credits with helping to shape his personality. Growing up in a rural area meant there weren't many other Black people around. He believes Ireland has come a long way since he was young and become a lot more open to the idea of Black people being Irish.

Dami's love of fashion started with a passion for sneakers. From there he developed his sense of style and built his whole wardrobe. He learned how to use his sneakers to dress up or down. Fashion was a form of expression that allowed him to show his personality. He believes that fashion is about projecting the way you want other people to see you. His major style influences were innovators like Kanye West and the American designer Virgil Abloh. He was also big into movies and would use fashion to step into some of his favourite characters.

Dami has a strong spiritual side and finds a lot of strength and comfort in God. For him, God has given him all that he has wanted: the ability to provide for his family on a level he never imagined possible.

Going on *Love Island* was a huge moment in Dami's life. He was popular on the show and regularly trended on socials. He met his now girlfriend, Indiyah, on the show, and they gave viewers some iconic moments during their

Camillat Mashaun

Camillat Mashaun, better known by her business name FreeBornNoble, is a businesswoman and entrepreneur from North Dublin. FreeBornNoble Hair is a Black-owned business that is now thriving in Ireland.

Camillat got started as an influencer showing the many styles you can create with wigs, before making it a full-time business. Her profile rose quickly after styling wigs for Yewande Biala, the first Black Irish woman to go on *Love Island*.

After sorting a second wig for Yewande during her time in the villa, Camillat stayed in touch with the show's make-up artist. Not long after, she was brought onto the *Love Island* team, and she styled wigs for contestant Kaz Kamwi. After this her business took off and is now putting the Irish wig game on the map.

time on the island. After finishing third, he left the house with a new-found celebrity status.

Dami says there are pros and cons to being a celebrity. He has received messages from fans that have told him he has inspired them, which he loves to hear. But he lives in a world where online trolls are a constant issue. He struggles to understand how people can go online and show hate or disrespect towards other people for no reason.

As a celebrity, Dami feels constant pressure to keep up with socials and ensure he is giving the value that his audience followed him for. It is hard work to keep himself visible. Dami feels like not enough people talk about this this side of public life. He appreciates his fans so much and loves that they support him. He understands that they may want to see him post all the time, but there are days when he wants to relax or focus on other things. He feels it's important to keep himself in check and make sure he's always taking care of himself. For Dami, it's helpful that he has a girlfriend who understands the pressures of celebrity life.

Dami isn't the only Black Irish person to have appeared on *Love Island*, though he is the first man. Other contestants have included Yewande Biala, Salma Naran and 2023's Catherine Agbaje.

Despite his TV success and celebrity profile, Dami's proudest moments are to do with his education and academic career. He holds a degree in microbiology. He worked in a lab where he became the head of his department and was able to build his own team. This was a big moment for him. Dami feels most proud of himself when he makes his friends or family proud.

Dami's advice to young and up-and-coming influencers is to know and be persistent with your craft. He believes in quality in your work: you need to ensure you're providing value to your followers. He doesn't believe in putting out content for the sake of it. Dami wants to see influencers who innovate and create. For him, copying trends is fine but it is also important to bring new ideas to your craft. You need to open your mind and not narrow yourself to one set of ideas.

Dami's official social media profiles have big followings. He is @damihope on both Instagram (more than 770k followers) and TikTok (more than 460k followers).

Dami also believes it's important to love and enjoy what you do and to have a community of friends and family that support you. Becoming an influencer isn't easy, but networking well can make it easier. Never be afraid to make new friends.

Dami's hope for the future of Ireland is that people like him no longer have to experience the many ways that racism presents itself. He hopes that the people of Ireland continue to unite against hatred, whether towards race, age, gender or sexuality. Lastly, he hopes that the restaurant Charlie's never goes out of business. These are things we can all get behind!

Acknowledgements

BRIANA

The first person I need to thank is my husband Paul, not just for shouldering the heavy lifting of parenting the kiddos while I was working away on this book, but also for his unwavering support for all of my work. To Gwen and Izzy, I know Mom's been busy, but this is all for you and for your future, which I hope is better than my past. The three of you hold my heart and have all my love, always. To my parents, Yvonne and Gene, thank you for encouraging me to pursue my love of writing from an early age and for always supporting me to follow my dreams. I hope that I have made you and all who came before us proud.

To my co-writer, Leon, thanks for trusting me with this. It's been a blast making your dreams a reality. To our publisher/editor extraordinaire, Matthew, you took the ideas and made them sparkle – thank you. And to Jessica, thank you for your beautiful artwork that will bring these stories to life for so many readers. To the Black and Irish team, especially Pierre, Jacinta and Benita, thanks for being the absolute best teammates and colleagues and for pitching in to help get this book made.

And finally, to the Legends, Trailblazers and Everyday Heroes in these pages: Black and Irish wouldn't exist without all of you and neither would this book. Thank you for all that you have done and all that you will do to make this world a more accepting place for future generations.

LEON

I'd like to thank my family, who supported me in writing this book. To my fiancée, Katie, who always spurred me on. To my parents, Rachel and Mark, and my siblings, Adam, Megan, Hollie, Rhea, Chloe and Jade. To my goddaughter and niece, Dolcee, who inspires me to work hard every day. To Katie's family, John, Debbie and Aoife, who have supported me while writing this book. Thank you. I love you all so very much.

To the Black and Irish team who have shown nothing but unwavering commitment to the Black and Irish community and its advancement in Irish society, thank you. For all you do and for all you give. It has been the honour of my life working with you. To my co-author Briana, thank you for all your work on this book, for your leadership and devotion to the cause. Black and Irish would not be where it is today without you.

To our publishers, Little Island, for your devotion to young readers and commitment to our cause, thank you. Your leadership throughout this publishing process has been admirable and we are so grateful to you. To Matthew Parkinson-Bennett, thank you for all you have done. Thank you for your patience, kindness, understanding and above all else your vision for this book that consistently steered us in the right direction.

To all those who bravely contributed to this book, thank you for sharing your story. You are all legends, you are all trailblazers and you are all everyday heroes. You have brought so much impact to the lives of others. We want this book to be a reminder of all you have achieved and what powerful humans you are.

ABOUT BRIANA FITZSIMONS

Briana Fitzsimons grew up in Yonkers, NY, USA, and has lived in Ireland since 2017. She has been a secondary school teacher for 12 years and also holds degrees in English and Creative Writing. Briana joined the Black and Irish team in 2021 and has been working to make schools across the country more inclusive for all students ever since. One of her main goals is to empower teachers and young people with the tools they need to make sure that everyone is seen and heard and feels a sense of belonging in all educational spaces in Ireland. She lives in County Kildare with her partner and two children and is proud to call Ireland home. She currently serves on the board of Inclusion Ireland.

ABOUT LEON DIOP

Leon Diop is a 28-year-old mixed-race man from Tallaght, Dublin, Ireland. Born to an Irish mother and a Senegalese father, he grew up in a mixed ethnic and religious household. He studied Psychology in Maynooth University where he served two years as Students' Union President. He is the founder of Black and Irish, an organisation striving to transform Ireland into a global leader in equality and inclusion. He is a host of the Black and Irish podcast with Irish national broadcaster, RTÉ. He currently serves on the boards of the Childhood Development Initiative, Tallaght, Work Equal and South Dublin County Partnership.

ABOUT JESSICA LOUIS

Jessica Louis is an independent Nigerian illustrator whose work features bright, colourful characters, shapes and scenes that speak to the emotions at the edges and at the core of our lived experience. She has exhibited with DesignOpp in Dublin and Fresco in Paris and been published in *Totally Dublin*. She's represented by Studio BLVCK and together they are paving a new path for independent black creatives across the world.

ABOUT BLACK AND IRISH

Black and Irish is an organisation that works to make Ireland more inclusive. They began telling the stories of Black and Mixed-Race people in Ireland in June 2020, in order to bring authentic discussion to Ireland around race and racism and tackle some of the issues that Black people experienced. Today the organisation works across six key areas of Irish society: education, business, politics, media, community and entertainment. Across these areas, Black and Irish aims to build a cohesive community, integrate that community into wider Irish society and reveal, challenge and eradicate racism in Irish society.

**black
& irish**

ABOUT LITTLE ISLAND

Little Island is an award-winning independent Irish publisher of books for young readers, founded in Dublin in 2010 by Ireland's first Laureate na nÓg (children's laureate), Siobhán Parkinson. Little Island books are found throughout Ireland, the UK, North America, and in translation around the world. You can find out more at littleisland.ie

RECENT AWARDS FOR LITTLE ISLAND BOOKS

White Raven winner 2023
The Kirkus Prize finalist 2023
Carnegie Medal for Writing shortlist 2023
YA Book Prize shortlist 2023
Branford Boase Award shortlist 2023
Great Reads Award shortlist 2023
The Eternal Return of Clara Hart by Louise Finch

USBBY (United States Board on Books for Young People) Outstanding International Books List 2023
Spark! School Book Award 2022: Fiction ages 9+
Wolfstongue by Sam Thompson

An Post Irish Book Awards shortlists 2023
Black & Irish: Legends, Trailblazers & Everyday Heroes
by Leon Diop and Briana Fitzsimons, illustrated by Jessica Louis
I Am the Wind: Irish Poems for Children Everywhere,
edited by Lucinda Jacob and Sarah Webb, illustrated by Ashwin Chacko
The Girl Who Fell to Earth by Patricia Forde
The Slug and the Snail by Oein DeBhairduin, illustrated by Olya Anima

Little
Island
Books create waves